Controve
Issues in
Educatic
Policy

CONTROVERSIAL ISSUES IN PUBLIC POLICY

Series Editors
Dennis Palumbo and Rita Mae Kelly
Arizona State University

Controversial Issues in Educational Policy

Louann A. Bierlein

Controversial Issues in Public Policy
Volume 4

SAGE Publications
International Educational and Professional Publisher
Newbury Park   London   New Delhi

For information address:

SAGE Publications, Inc.
2455 Teller Road
Newbury Park, California 91320

SAGE Publications Ltd.
6 Bonhill Street
London EC2A 4PU
United Kingdom

SAGE Publications India Pvt. Ltd.
M-32 Market
Greater Kailash I
New Delhi 110 048 India

Printed in the United States of America

Library of Congress Cataloging-in-Publication Data

Bierlein, Louann A.
  Controversial issues in educational policy / Louann A. Bierlein.
    p.   cm.—(Controversial issues in public policy ; v. 4)
  Includes bibliographical references (p.   ) and index.
  ISBN 0-8039-4832-8.—ISBN 0-8039-4833-6 (pbk.)
  1. Education and state—United States.   2. Education—United
States—Aims and objectives.   3. School, Choice of—United States.
I. Title. II. Series.
LC89.B49   1993
379.73—dc20   92-30570
                                                                  CIP

93 94 95 96   10 9 8 7 6 5 4 3 2 1

Sage Production Editor: Judith L Hunter

Contents

Acknowledgments

I want to thank a number of individuals who have enriched this book through their support and ideas. First, my husband, best friend, and first-line editor, Tim Palmer. Second, Lori Mulholland, my research assistant, who literally fell into my life at the right moment and for whom I am greatly indebted. Third, my director and mentor, Rob Melnick, for his encouragement and for allowing me to tap into resources at the Morrison Institute for Public Policy, Arizona State University. Fourth, to several colleagues who have spent many hours with me working to improve Arizona's educational public policies: Judy Richardson, former Senator Jacque Steiner, Kim Sheane, Nancy Mendoza, Martha Dorsey, Senator Bev Hermon, and Senator Lela Alston. Finally, to my parents and family, who instilled in me a strong work ethic without which little would have been accomplished.

Series Editors' Introduction

Public policy controversies escalated during the 1980s and early 1990s. This was partly due to bitter partisan debate between Republicans and Democrats, a "divided" government in which the Republicans controlled the Presidency and the Democrats controlled the Congress, and the rise of "negative" campaigning in the 1988 presidential election. In addition, the past decade was a time when highly controversial issues such as abortion, crime, environmental pollution, affirmative action and choice in education became prominent on the public policy agenda.

Policy issues in this atmosphere tend to be framed in dichotomous, either-or terms. Abortion is depicted as "murder" on the one hand, or a woman's "self-interested choice" on the other. One is either "tough" on crime, or too much in favor of "defendants' rights." Affirmative action is a matter of "quotas" or a special interest issue. School choice is a means for correcting the "educational mess," or the destruction of public education. In such a situation there doesn't seem to be a middle or common ground where cooler heads can unite.

The shrillness of these policy disputes reduces the emphasis on finding rational, balanced solutions. Political ideology and a zero-sum approach to politics and policy became the order of the day.

Certainly, there hasn't been an "end to ideology" over the past decade and a half as some have believed was occurring in the 1970s. "Reaganomics" contributed to a widening gap between the rich and the poor during the 1980s and this seemed to exacerbate partisan debate and further stymie governmental action. In 1992, controversies over health care—lack of coverage for millions and skyrocketing costs—illustrate the wide gap in the way Republicans and Democrats approach public policy controversies. The Reagan "revolution" was based on a definite and clear ideological preference for a certain approach to public policy in general: eliminate government regulation; reduce taxes; provide tax incentives for business; cut welfare; and privatize the delivery of governmental services. Democrats, of course, did not agree.

This series in Public Policy Controversies is meant to shed more light and less ideological heat on major policy issues in the substantive policy areas. Louann Bierlein begins this volume by noting that controversy is the norm rather than the exception in education. This is because the system has tried to simultaneously fulfill the conflicting goals of equity, efficiency, choice and excellence. Moreover, the two principal ideologies of conservatism and liberalism combine these values in different ways. She shows how these ideologies are reflected in the various policy debates.

After describing the historical development of education, she goes on to note that the ideal of equity has not been achieved because of the emphasis on the "right" of local taxpayers to supplement state revenues. And there is a question about whether money does make a difference in student outcomes.

Perhaps it is the way schools are run; like factories, they have uniform working conditions with centralized educational bureaucracies. However, not everyone agrees with these criticisms. It may well be that the system needs a complete overhaul, but there is no agreement on what that overhaul should be.

It is difficult to hold schools accountable, Bierlein notes, because it is impossible to develop bias-free mental measurements. So it may be impossible to tell when schools are getting better even if they are completely restructured. Choice, of course, was the principal item on the agenda in 1992 as a way of improving the system, and Bierlein examines the issue thoroughly and dispassionately. The likelihood is that states will implement public school choice as a way of holding off private school forces.

Bierlein concludes by asking, "Can schools do it all?" Readers will, we believe, find Bierlein's answers and discussion illuminating, well-reasoned, thoroughly researched, and good reading.

RITA MAE KELLY
DENNIS PALUMBO

1

The American Educational System
How Has It Come to Be?

Everyone Is an Expert

Americans have long considered education a top priority. From the spread of the common school system in the 1830s to higher education's near universal access in the 1990s, the United States is known for providing the most egalitarian educational system in the world. Education is viewed as important to "getting ahead" and achieving the opportunities life offers—an equalizer across economic and social lines. As our forefathers believed, education is fundamental to the preservation of a democratic society. Indeed, when the nation's superiority or economic vitality is threatened, education becomes a focal point. When the Russian satellite Sputnik was launched in 1957 and when the auto industry began crumbling in the 1980s, people turned to the educational system, laying both their anger and their hopes at its feet. A love/hate relationship has long existed between Americans and education, the system that uses so much of their tax money, yet represents the backbone of their communities.

The elementary and secondary educational system (i.e., K-12) is sizable. In the fall of 1989, more than 46 million K-12 students were enrolled in American public and private schools; 88% of these students were in public schools, with the remaining 12% in private schools. Approximately 2.8 million people were employed as schoolteachers; other professional, administrative, and support staff numbered 2.4 million. In total, more than 51 million Americans, or one of every five, were directly or indirectly involved in providing or receiving K-12 education during 1989, costing more that $215 billion, or 4.1% of the nation's gross national product (National Center for Education Statistics, 1991a).

Because most Americans have been through the system, nearly all believe they are "experts." Few people feel qualified to criticize the medical or engineering profession; they may not like attorneys, but they seldom advise them how to practice law. The public does not know the terminology or the practice of these other professions, while nearly everyone feels comfortable offering advice on how to improve the educational system. It is commonly heard: "If only they would go back to teaching the way I was taught—back to the basics." Of course, few realize that when they were in school many more students were dropping out than currently. Indeed, more students are graduating today, having obtained higher levels of knowledge than ever before (Berliner, 1992). Many citizens want a return to the basics, but they also want art, music, computers, sex education, foreign language, athletics, vocational education, and a dozen other topics taught. Multiple constituencies need to be served, each wanting education to fulfill its version of the American dream. While education continues to be the hope for America's ills, it also serves as a focal point for public debate and criticism.

This book highlights many current education public policy issues being debated at the White House, in statehouses, at meetings of local school boards, and among corporate leaders. Examining the history of these issues will illustrate underlying principles and waves of reform, as driven by larger demographic, societal, and economic influences. Over time, the pendulum between conservatism and liberalism has often swung back and forth while many issues that seem settled have resurfaced. The purpose of this book is to overview many controversial issues, not to provide an in-depth analysis of any given issue. Conscious effort was made not to provide answers, but to review the many sides of each issue.

Is there a right or wrong within the educational policy debates, and will people ever reach consensus? As part of our pluralist society,

Weiler (1990) writes, "Educational policy has shown a particular propensity for conflict. Few policy issues . . . have generated as much controversy in as wide a variety of settings as education, especially in situations where major changes in education policy were proposed" (p. 440). Education is the principal instrument through which societies pass on values and norms to future generations of citizens. Given the disagreement over the desired nature of social relations and the normative bases of human and social behavior, education will always remain susceptible to conflict. Acknowledging that controversy is the norm rather than the exception, the review begins.

Values and Ideologies in Conflict

Four underlying societal values drive debates within the educational policy arena and will be examined throughout this book: equity, efficiency, liberty, and excellence. *Equity,* or egalitarianism, focuses on providing equal education opportunity for all children. *Efficiency* looks at utilizing resources to their full potential (i.e., increasing output per unit of input). *Liberty* or choice concerns an individual's right to choose from among different courses of action, to maintain local control of decisions. *Excellence* involves producing a high-quality product, not necessarily at the lowest cost, but the best. These are conditions that most Americans want maximized, and against which policy processes and products are judged; they are deeply rooted in our heritage. However, the simultaneous fulfillment of these values is almost impossible. Exclusive pursuit of one violates or eliminates another; attention to balance is necessary but difficult due to multiple constituencies. Thus, various waves of educational reform have been driven by pressures to focus on one principle to the exclusion of others.

For example, during the 1930s a primary focus was on streamlining the educational system through scientific management principles. Centralized bureaucratic structures were created, improving the efficiency of schooling but decreasing liberty or individual choice within the system. During the 1960s and 1970s providing equal educational opportunities for all students was vital since segregation had caused many schools to be inferior. Many federal laws protecting the rights of individual students ensued, but these laws also restricted local governing boards' freedom of choice in running their districts. Districts also focused on the minimums that every child should learn, thereby sacrificing excellence. Finally, statewide achievement testing and increased graduation standards during the 1980s were meant to achieve excellence, but in many cases were not egalitarian and proved to be an inefficient use of resources.

Going one step further, two general ideologies—conservatism and liberalism—combine these four values in unique ways, blending those associated with democracy (e.g., equity) with those linked to capitalism (e.g., liberty). Distinctions between the two views are subtle and complex, yet Tyll van Geel (1991) indicates that *conservatism* embodies the free market system as the preferable economic system, even though capitalism will inevitably produce social, economic, and political inequalities. Within this view, government should not aggressively seek to redistribute wealth and eliminate inequalities; primary control of education should rest with the states, not the federal government or the courts. Finally, state and local governments have a special function to "shape" children, to bring them into the local community and make them good citizens, and to socialize them and inculcate "American" and community values.

On the other side, the goal of *liberalism* is to enhance social equality, specifically for the poor and the powerless, through reliance on a strong central government. Education plays an important role by ameliorating the social inequalities arising from the market system; expanding opportunities for all students, liberating the mind; and preparing students for active participation in a robust, democratic, secular political process.

A conservative view, therefore, encourages an educational system with limited (or no) government control in order to maximize individual choices. A primary role of education is to inculcate American values as expeditiously as possible. Generally, conservatives support parental choice of public or private schools, but they resist bilingual education programs that maintain a student's first language and culture while learning English. They also seek to have schools fulfill a more narrow role, with a primary focus on academics. Conversely, liberals prefer an educational system with strong government oversight to ensure equal protection for all students despite the loss of individual choice. Their ideal system capitalizes on our society's diversity and supports programs such as bilingual education. Liberals also favor a broader role of schooling, including vocational and self-esteem programs.

Public policy involves a weave of these beliefs and values and is dependent upon the social and economic climate. Except for those at the extreme far left or right, the views of most people on a given issue will be a blend of conservative and liberal ideals. Throughout this book, opposite sides of an issue are frequently offered to show the extremes; however, this is not to imply that all people categorically believe in one view or the other (i.e., that people are either liberal or conservative). In actuality, many individuals will incorporate aspects of each extreme into their viewpoint on a given issue (i.e., moderates). As the reader will see, many educational issues involve interactions and tradeoffs; conflicts or controversies are the net result.

Historical Origins

The first step in understanding current controversial education issues is a brief review of the foundations of the American educational system and of cycles of reform as the societal value pendulum has swung between two extreme ideologies. Subsequent chapters will provide additional historical detail as relevant to a given issue. Michael Kirst (1984) of Stanford University writes:

> Americans have always believed that education policy is too important to leave to educators. Now, as in the past, an aroused citizenry can powerfully influence school policy. But education policy is a complex subject. To be effective in shaping policy requires a sophisticated understanding of the history of education and of current patterns of control. Without such an understanding, today's aroused citizens may become frustrated citizens, unprepared for the complexities they must face. (p. xiii)

Pre-1800s

The tradition of local control (i.e., liberty) can be traced to the very beginning of our country. Having left a highly centralized Church of England, the Puritans abhorred concentrated authority and insisted on local congregational autonomy. As the first formal education law, the "Old Deluder Satan Act" of 1647 required every Massachusetts town of at least 50 families to hire a teacher, setting the precedent of public responsibility for education as overseen by the local community. However, schooling was restricted to a few years' instruction in basic skills with the primary goal of having children being able to read the Bible.

Only sons of the upper classes attended highly academic secondary schools, preparing them for political leadership or the ministry.

During the middle and late 1700s, intellectual leaders such as Thomas Jefferson argued that political stability was enhanced by widespread knowledge. At the Constitutional Convention in 1787, he emphasized that no free nation could survive ignorance. Although most agreed with the need to expand educational opportunity, debates ensued as to whether there should be a national system of education or one of state and local control. Many believed in public funding of religious schools, while others were adamant that separation of church and state was essential for a free democracy. Out of these conflicts came support for a system of locally controlled and funded, nonsectarian public schools. However, the system at this time still comprised only a few years for many white children, and advanced schooling for the elite few.

Schooling for the Masses—The System Grows

The 1830s brought the rise of the "common school" belief. Advocated by men such as Horace Mann, the goal was to develop a publicly financed elementary education system for the masses. Unlike Jefferson, who believed in minimal schooling for all and additional education for the elite, Mann declared that an educated citizenry would improve the standard of living for all. Education was to be the springboard of opportunity and would equalize diversity among people from different social classes. A vast social movement supporting the common school concept spread across the country; by 1860, more than 50% of the nation's children were enrolled in school. States gave local communities the authority and responsibility for the operation and financing of schools whereby property taxes became the major means of support. In addition, a major expansion of higher education institutions occurred, in part to meet the growing need for public schoolteachers. Many existing state universities originated as "normal schools," or teacher training institutions, initially providing only 1 or 2 years of formal training.

The rise of secondary education for the masses and the need for a more comprehensive curriculum also began to occur. Prior to 1830 several private boys' academies with a strong academic focus existed, but few public high schools had been established. However, large numbers of immigrants requiring both work skills and an orientation to the values of the country led communities to build and support free public high schools. As these schools grew, so did the debate over the curricula to be provided.

Some professional educators argued that the primary task of secondary education was to develop and discipline students' minds through a strong academic curriculum, even if most students did not go on to higher education. However, pressure by business leaders supporting vocational education, and the overwhelming task of educating large numbers of immigrant students, represented competing forces. As a result, Congress passed the Smith-Hughes Act of 1918, providing federal support for vocational education programs. In addition, a group of leading educators published "The Cardinal Principles of Secondary Education," stating that high school curriculum was to focus on "health, worthy home membership, vocation, citizenship, worthy use of leisure time, and ethical character" (Kirst, 1984, p. 36). A noticeable absence was the focus on academic excellence.

Using the Cardinal Principles as a guide, most high schools became utilitarian in nature, with academics being retained for the small elite group seeking higher education. Toch (1991) indicates that these principles were adopted because many educators assumed that immigrant students surging into the schools were incapable of mastering academic subject matter. Advocates of intelligence testing asserted that those scoring below 100 were destined for no more than clerical labor and that at least 80% of the immigrants were "feeble-minded." Using tests based on these beliefs, systems of sorting and tracking were established during the early 1900s to more efficiently handle the sea of new students. Few people realized the bias these tests contained against children with limited English proficiency.

The Depression Era (1930-1941) expanded the need for public education. The lack of jobs and the view that education would provide job opportunities resulted in many additional students attending secondary schools. In 1930 there were approximately 5 million high school students; by 1941 there were more than 6.5 million and, as shown in Figure 1.1, for the first time more than half were graduating. This era also saw the development of "progressive education," where many opposed the traditional teaching methods requiring children to sit in rows, reciting as they are called upon. Instead, these progressives believed that children should learn by doing and through critical thinking. Using the work of John Dewey, they moved to democratize the masses by rewriting the curriculum, focusing on students' day-to-day experiences and reflecting

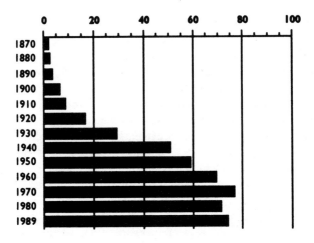

Figure 1.1. High School Graduates (1870-1989) (as a percent of 17-year-old population)
SOURCE: Department of Education, National Center for Statistics, *Digest of Education Statistics* (Washington, DC: Government Printing Office, 1990), p. 108.

more fully the diversity of life. Although Dewey believed that these principles should be integrated into a strong academic curriculum, the prevailing view was that democracy would be served best by offering usable studies to everyone, instead of dwelling on academics of interest to only a few. The Progressive crusade also worked to alleviate urban slum conditions caused by industrialization and mass immigration. Lessons in hygiene, nutrition, and child care were soon part of schooling, thanks to the egalitarian social concerns of the period. The framework for comprehensive public high schools, providing both academic and practical life and workplace skills, was firmly in place.

Peacetime social life and economic expansion followed World War II, bringing an even more liberal view to schooling. Enrollments continued to grow and "life-adjustment" programs of the 1940s were developed to help society as a whole make the transition from war to peace (Kirst, 1984). Systematic attention to intellectual rigor or subject content was avoided; life values were placed above the acquisition of knowledge (Armstrong, Henson, & Savage, 1985; Toch, 1991). The pendulum had swung even more strongly to the nonacademic side. Overall, schooling was fairly peaceful as the economy continued to grow, challenged only by conservative groups concerned with the lack of academic excellence for the masses.

The First International Scare

Complacency, however, was short-lived, as several events in the 1950s shook America's confidence in its educational system. In 1954 the Supreme Court reversed its nineteenth-century *Plessy v. Ferguson* decision and ruled, in *Brown v. Board of Education of Topeka,* that segregated schools were inherently unequal. This court case spotlighted the dismal conditions of schooling for minorities and set the stage for expanded federal intervention. The Soviet launching of Sputnik in 1957 further electrified the world—the Russians were winning the space race. Americans blamed the public schools for this failure since academic instruction in public schools was believed inferior to that of other countries. In response, Congress passed the National Defense Education Act of 1957, providing millions of dollars for math, science, and foreign language education. Thousands of teachers were trained, and highly academic science and math curricula were written. Programs for gifted students were encouraged, and the pendulum swung quickly toward academic excellence. However, as America quickly reestablished its technological superiority over the Soviets, the drive for stronger academics subsided. The focal point instead became concern over equity, as initiated by the *Brown* decision and expanded by the Civil Rights Act of 1964.

The 1960s and early 1970s saw a wave of student dissatisfaction and a focus on unequal social conditions. President Lyndon B. Johnson's War on Poverty was firmly established with the passage of the $1.5-billion Elementary and Secondary Education Act in 1965. As schools turned to providing equal educational opportunities for poor and minority students, schools placed many of these students into remedial courses, building on traditions begun decades earlier. Even civil-rights activists argued that forcing disadvantaged students into demanding academic courses would discriminate against children already suffering the consequences of other discrimination. Concurrent with the federal focus on equity-type programs, students themselves became a vocal constituency expressing alienation from adults and dissatisfaction with school curricula. Fueled by the Vietnam war and a resurgence of progressive, child-centered views, students demanded more relevance and individual choice. In response, graduation requirements were eliminated and a "shopping mall" selection of electives was offered. Innovation became the watchword with team-teaching, open classrooms, and performance-contracting on the agenda. In addition, federal efforts to ensure equal access for handicapped, limited English proficient (LEP), minority, and female students evolved into strict federal and state laws protecting these populations. Civil-rights, student-rights, teacher-rights, and equity issues dominated the educational system during this time. Many believed these activities came at the expense of academic excellence.

During the late 1970s and early 1980s, a growing number of conservative education critics gained recognition. Toch (1991) notes that these critics "attacked the educational liberalism of the 1960s and 1970s that discouraged the teaching of rigorous academic subjects to many students. They were harshly critical of public education's response to the civil rights and antipoverty movements of the 1960s, arguing that education policy makers . . . had overemphasized issues of educational access at the expense of the quality of education" (p. 56). Due in part to federal requirements, states attempted to ensure that all students met at least minimal academic skills. Basic skills tests were initiated, and, as explored in Chapter 4, these "minimums" frequently became the "maximums." As comprehensive test data became available, national news reports surfaced on the failures of schooling. In 1975 it was disclosed that average Scholastic Aptitude Test (SAT) scores had been falling for the previous 11 years. American businesses, already feeling the economic pressures from the growing Japanese market, spoke of inadequate skills and difficulty in finding qualified workers. The media spotlighted barely literate people who had obtained high school diplomas. "Back to basics" was advocated by many. Overall citizen dissatisfaction with schools (and government in general) resulted in a wave of tax limitation initiatives across the nation, with California's Proposition 13 perhaps the most widely discussed in the media. In total, tax or expenditure limitations were adopted in 17 states between 1976 and 1980 (Guthrie, Garms, & Pierce, 1988). The pendulum had quickly swung again toward the conservative side.

The Current Reforms

By the early 1980s the educational debates had made national headlines. President Ronald Reagan advocated the use of private school vouchers to free parents from weak public school systems. Many state policymakers began their push for excellence by increasing graduation requirements and upgrading teacher certification standards. Numerous national commissions were established to study the issue. None, however, had the impact of *A Nation At Risk: The Imperative for Educational Reform,* a report released in 1983 by Secretary of Education Terrell Bell. Its chilling opening words warned:

> Our Nation is at risk. Our once unchallenged preeminence in commerce, industry, science, and technological innovation is being overtaken by competitors throughout the world. . . . the educational foundations of our society are presently being eroded by a rising tide of mediocrity that threatens our very future as a Nation and a people. . . . If an unfriendly power had attempted to impose on America the mediocre educational performance that exists today, we might have viewed it as an act of war. (National Commission on Excellence in Education, 1983, p. 5)

The highly publicized report fueled educational reform debates. By 1986, 35 states had enacted educational reform legislation; nearly a dozen had raised taxes to support activities; many had raised graduation requirements, instituted performance-based pay programs, increased teacher testing, developed internships for first-year teachers, and strengthened teacher certification and accreditation rules (Brown Easton, 1991). Many of these reforms were, and continue to be, extremely controversial.

Although considerable money and energy were spent on improving academic excellence in the 1980s, conservatives hasten to point out that little evidence of real progress exists. While slight improvements have occurred in SAT scores since all-time lows in 1979 through 1981, current scores are far from those attained in the early 1960s. And while minority students have made tremendous gains, as evidenced by test scores and graduation rates compared to 1960s data, their overall school successes remain far behind those of non-minority students (Smith & O'Day, 1991). Liberals challenge that growing poverty rates and societal turmoil offset any changes the system is trying to make. Some note that current assessments cannot measure higher skill outcomes and that more students are staying in school, thereby increasing the pool of test-takers (i.e., more than an elite few taking the test). Conservatives contend that the reforms of the 1980s excellence movement simply attempted to deal with symptoms, not causes, of public education's problems. From their perspective, the agrarian, 9-month, 6-hour-per-day system, even with better trained and more highly motivated teachers, can accomplish only so much. In addition, most 1980s reforms were "top-down" standardized efforts to force quick, presumably efficient changes.

Utilizing many principles adopted by American corporations that also lost economic superiority, the second wave of the excellence movement began during the late 1980s. Current reforms focus on school restructuring, site-based decision making, new forms of accountability, and the development of market-niche schools. Emphasis is also being placed on the disadvantaged or at-risk students; but unlike with the programs of the 1960s, equity is being redefined to mean equal outcomes, not simply equal access. The goal is to create an American system that for the first time truly attempts to educate all students to their fullest potential. Many now realize that the tracking and sorting of disadvantaged students in the past served no one. Although reforms of the 1980s were controversial, they only attempted to improve the system; the reforms of the 1990s are trying to build a new system. Controversy abounds.

During the 1980s and into the 1990s, education has become a top political agenda at both state and national levels. Many have laid claim to being an "education president" or "education governor." Formal national educational goals have been established for the first time in our history, and President George Bush's *America 2000* efforts have tried to focus state attention on attaining these goals. Numerous business organizations, such as the National Alliance of Business, the Committee for Economic Development, and the Business Roundtable, plus groups such as the National Governors' Association, are attempting to marshal great societal forces in order to recreate our system of education—one balancing the principles of equity, efficiency, liberty, and excellence. This has never existed, and most agree it will be difficult if not impossible to accomplish.

Strong business involvement has added a new dimension to the education policy debates. Because free enterprise is one foundation of American society, many uphold that school ills can be cured by operating education "like a business." For example, proposals to improve the efficiency of the system, as well as the final product—the student—are inherent in the call for increased parental choice and market forces. Policymakers are taking steps to either allow or require school systems to move decision making closer to the school (i.e., site-based management), a practice with its origin in business. Many legislators and corporate leaders want teacher compensation to be based on performance, similar to the private sector. Indeed, education is perhaps the largest single "business" in the nation in terms of its resources and personnel, and many believe a great deal can be learned from sound business practices.

However, it is important to recognize key organizational differences between the educational system and private business. As noted by the National Alliance of Business (1990):

> [There are] differences in organizational culture between business and education, specifically their different roles in and ties to American life, their different managerial philosophies, their different governing contexts and their different organizational structures. Business and education do not share identical concerns or see the same world, speak the same language, and, even more importantly, share similar values. . . . Today's successful businesses have adapted to the changed environment, new technology, and changing markets; they can help schools do the same. But, they must take care to work with educators to be sure that their successful actions in the private sector are adapted to the education environment. (p. 5-6)

Although the differences noted in Figure 1.2 are often viewed by critics as excuses, they are real; and in many cases, little can be done to change certain aspects of the educational system (e.g., open meeting laws, locally elected governing boards). Most national reform leaders have accepted these differences and are working with educators to rebuild a system within given organizational constraints. Unfortunately, others still either do not understand or refuse to accept the differences between education and business. Policymakers seeking to reform education, as well as those analyzing educational public policies, need to understand the organizational and legal constraints on public education in order to minimize conflicts and maximize the probability of success.

In Review

Our system of public education is a fairly young enterprise. Prior to the common school movement in the 1830s, only a small percentage of American children had access to anything other than the basics. As shown previously, it was not until 1940 that more than half of America's high school students graduated. This was barely 50 years ago. It is difficult to point to a time in our history when the educational system

BUSINESS SECTOR	EDUCATION SECTOR
■ Powerful and autonomous chief executive and board of directors	■ Chief executive operating under contraints imposed by independent state and local boards and state officials
■ Can operate in relative privacy	■ A public institution, unable to limit media or citizen access
■ Can totally restructure by closing plants, changing products, changing markets, etc.	■ Must continue to provide education services to all clientele
■ Incentives and sanctions are accepted aspects of performance evaluation	■ No existing rewards (or sanctions) structure for good (or poor) performance
■ Can determine its organizational structure	■ Has limited organizational flexibility
■ Can shape its public image through media relations	■ Has few or no promotional resources
■ Can access state-of-the-art technology	■ Has few resources to keep technology current
■ Can implement and enforce quality control standards for its goods and services	■ Difficult and complex to assess and measure a "quality" education
■ Can target its products and select its consumers	■ Must serve all students assigned to it

Figure 1.2. Differences Between the Business and Education Sectors

SOURCE: National Alliance of Business, *Business Strategies That Work: A Planning Guide for Education Restructuring* (Washington, DC, 1990), p. 6. Reprinted with permission.

has been static. It has been pulled in many directions by the ever-growing number of students, the desire of society to have a comprehensive program of study, and strong political and economic forces.

Kirst (1984) notes that during periods of conservative political movements such as the 1890s, the late 1950s, and the early 1980s, education reform focused on academic standards and traditional subjects such as English, math, and history. During periods of economic liberalism or progressive movements, such as the Depression and the 1960s, the focus has been on opportunity, equality, and vocational preparation. Although education and the economy have been linked in the past, strong business interest and the evolving world economy may have firmly merged the two issues together for the foreseeable future. Already these forces have lengthened the current educational reform wave far longer than most had predicted. As stated in *A Nation At Risk* (1983):

> History is not kind to idlers. The time is long past when America's destiny was assured simply by an abundance of natural resources and inexhaustible human enthusiasm, and by our relative isolation from the malignant problems of older civilizations. The world is indeed one global village. We live among determined, well-educated, and strongly motivated competitors. . . . America's position in the world may once have been reasonably secure with only a few well-trained men and women. It is no longer. (p. 6)

Since this statement was written nearly a decade ago, the world has changed dramatically. The rise of the European Community, the reunification of Germany, the dismantling of the Soviet Union, the fall of communism, and the growing strength of many overseas markets serve to make these words more powerful. Our forefathers' goals of educating the masses have resulted in an egalitarian education system matched by no other country in the world. However, the world is not the same; and, just as American businesses have been forced to change, so must education. Creating a new system involving nearly 50 million K-12 students and teachers entails many conflicts, especially within a pluralist democratic society. Chapter 2 briefly reviews two additional facets of the current system—lines of control and resource equity—before moving on to the policy debates in subsequent chapters.

2

Who Is in Charge
and How Equal Are We?

Levels of Educational Control

In analyzing education policy debates, one needs to understand the public nature of the K-12 educational system and the tangled lines of authority and power. American school practices reflect compromises among local, state, and national forces involving *governmental* bodies (e.g., Congress, U.S. Department of Education, U.S. Supreme Court, governors, legislators, state boards of education, state departments of education, district governing boards, district administrators), as well as *nongovernmental* groups (e.g., teacher unions, parent-teacher associations, business organizations). Strong public interest in education, coupled with these formally organized entities, has yielded numerous constituencies. The tension among these varying interests produces conflict and ultimately a system where lines of control are blurred. Figure 2.1 highlights key governmental entities involved in education policy-making as well as the many outside nongovernmental groups that greatly impact the process. Brief sketches of the major players follow.

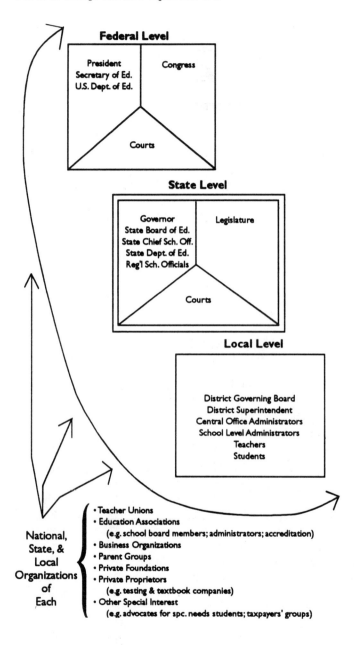

Figure 2.1. Educational Policy Influences

The National Level

The United States is nearly unique in not having a national system of schooling; instead, control is decentralized to the states. Although Australia, Canada, and West Germany also operate decentralized education systems, they are less dependent upon state and local school authorities than the United States. Having lived under a strong British monarchy, America's forefathers were reluctant to grant a single national entity the authority over something as influential as education, and therefore consciously chose to give this responsibility to the states. Consequently, Congress and the federal government have no formalized authority to operate education programs. Yet, they play a significant role in developing education policies that impact our country's system. How is this possible?

Implied powers within several provisions of the U.S. Constitution provide the federal government with limited authority to regulate the educational system. In addition, numerous U.S. Supreme Court interpretations have expanded these powers over time rather than limited them. Three specific provisions are important in understanding the federal role. First, the *general welfare clause* grants Congress the power to provide for the common defense and general welfare of the United States. This provision is used to defend activities attempting to meet unaddressed national needs (e.g., free/reduced lunch funding) and to perform functions logically falling to a central authority, even if they overshadow the role of the states (e.g., National Assessment of Educational Progress [NAEP] testing).

Second, the U.S. Supreme Court has held that language in the First Amendment was intended to create a wall of *separation between church and state*. Consistent with this view, both state and federal courts have struck down repeated efforts to provide direct financial subsidies to religious schools. Current interpretations allow only very restricted funds for some private school activities (e.g., limited student transportation, select federal programs). However, as current debates continue over instituting private school vouchers, many predict a new round of court challenges regarding the separation of church and state.

Third, the *equal protection clause* of the Fourteenth Amendment serves as the foundation for many policy debates. Using this clause, the U.S. Supreme Court's school desegregation decision in *Brown v. Board of Education of Topeka* fundamentally changed schooling in the South and, to a lesser degree, throughout the country. The declaration that "separate but equal" was unconstitutional opened the door to court-ordered desegregation and busing debates that still impact our system nearly 40 years later. The equal protection clause also serves as a foundation for debates and court challenges over school finance issues.

Beyond implied constitutional powers, Congress and the federal government wield considerable authority by holding the purse strings on significant sums of money. Programs administered by the U.S. Department of Education (and their 1990 funding levels) include: vocational and adult education ($908 million), compensatory education for the disadvantaged ($4.6 billion), bilingual education ($204 million), education for the handicapped ($1.7 billion), Indian education ($67 million), and school improvement programs ($1.26 billion). Major educational programs administered by other federal agencies include child nutrition programs ($5.5 billion), "Head Start" preschool programs ($1.4 billion), and training programs such as Job Corps ($2.3 billion). In total, these programs plus others represented more than $21 billion in federal funding for K-12 education during 1990 (National Center for Education Statistics, 1991a).

Although these funding amounts are significant, federal support covers only slightly more than 6% of total K-12 educational expenditures. Nonetheless, a plethora of federal regulations accompany these funds, greatly restricting local liberties and making effective use of such funding virtually impossible. Recent efforts have attempted to limit federal regulations; however, most contend that very few barriers have been removed. States have generally resigned themselves to this "big brother" role because federal funds help support many equity-type programs required by court actions (e.g., special education). However, few state policymakers are content with the situation, and ongoing federal versus state conflicts exist.

Finally, educational policy is affected by the agenda of the president in office and by the executive branch under the president's control (e.g., Secretary of Education, U.S. Department of Education). For example, fueled by increased public interest in education, President Ronald Reagan influenced many national educational policy debates. Appointing William Bennett Secretary of Education, advocating tuition tax credits, and waging war against bilingual education were several actions for which Reagan will be remembered. One primary goal of his administration was to instill the ideal of a new federalism, wherein states would assume responsibility for programs previously funded and controlled by the federal government. President George Bush has also laid claim to the "education president" title. Under his administration, more hands-on efforts are being taken to mobilize state action. Through his *America 2000* campaign, President Bush and Secretary of Education Lamar Alexander hope to fast-track educational reform. Their support for private school choice vouchers has also fueled that debate across the nation.

In sum, although the federal level has little formal authority over education, great power is wielded through funding and program regulations, Supreme Court decisions, and the presidential bully pulpit. However, many are now debating whether our country should have a more "nationalized" approach to education: that is, more formalized power to create uniformity among state policies. Notions such as a national curriculum and testing system have resurfaced and are being debated with vigor. Although these concepts were purposely shunned by our forefathers, today many believe that the entire system of education must be revamped to ensure America's economic vitality. Advocates believe a stronger national role would most efficiently accomplish this task. As a result, there is great tension between the notion of a new federalism and attempts to nationalize education. Further discussion of this issue is offered in Chapters 4 and 7.

The State Level

The Tenth Amendment specifies that powers not delegated to the federal government by the U.S. Constitution are to be reserved to the states, and therefore, education has become a state responsibility. In turn, provisions within each state constitution charge state legislators to maintain a free public education system. Large bodies of state laws have been enacted in an attempt to ensure that at least minimum resources are available and certain state standards are met. A separate legislative standing committee is usually dedicated to educational issues; some states have two committees, one each for K-12 education and higher education issues. Chairpersons of these committees as well as their legislative staff have great influence over state education policies. Considering that an average of 50% of K-12 public education is financed through state revenues, legislators feel a major oversight responsibility to state taxpayers.

In addition to legislative control, most states have an elected or appointed state board of education that governs the system, plus an elected or appointed state chief school officer (i.e., superintendent of public instruction or commissioner of education). It is the state chief school officer's responsibility to oversee a state department of education and to carry out the policies and statutes enacted by the legislature or the state board. Each state department of education also has the responsibility of distributing federal funding and ensuring state compliance with federal laws and regulations. Many states have regional or county school officials who operate intermediary agencies, some having control over local school districts, while others simply offer support services.

The amount of centralized authority over budget, personnel, and curriculum varies greatly among states. In some, strong state authority is maintained by the legislature and state board of education through control over teaching salary schedules and textbook selection. In others, "local control" means less state intervention in day-to-day operations; instead, broad guidelines are offered. During the reforms of the 1980s, most states, even those with historically strong local control, initiated many top-down initiatives. The reforms of the 1990s now call for states to provide more authority to individual districts and schools. For example, many states now allow waivers from state laws or regulations (other than health, safety, and due process) that would otherwise prevent local improvements. Chapter 3 provides additional information on the policy debates over the decentralization of decision-making authority.

State courts also play a key role in deciding cases that challenge the implementation of various laws (e.g., special education) or allege violation of certain constitutional provisions regarding free and appropriate education (e.g., school finance equity cases). The role of the courts in education policy-making is becoming even more prominent, as shown by the Kentucky Supreme Court's declaring the entire state K-12 educational system unconstitutional in 1989.

Finally, although historically minor players in educational policy, governors have been a major influence since the early 1980s. As education captured broad public attention, Republican and Democratic candidates alike saw education as a powerful political platform and a major link to economic recovery. No longer did governors limit their role to education executive appointments, but instead they hired education specialists as executive staff and developed comprehensive state reform plans. Many used their bully pulpit to convince state legislators and the public to support major reforms and increase revenues for education. Several governors have become recognized as leaders across the country for their efforts to reform education within their states: Bill

Clinton of Arkansas, Lamar Alexander of Tennessee, John Ascroft of Missouri, Dick Riley of South Carolina, and Bill Romer of Colorado, among others. Collectively, the National Governors' Association has focused a great deal of attention on educational issues. This organization has released several reports outlining key reform strategies and has been working closely with key business leaders, Congress, and the president's office to advocate for such reforms.

The Local Level

Just as the U.S. Constitution delegates full authority for education to the states, many states in turn assign much of their power to locally elected district governing boards (i.e., local school boards). Because most, if not all, K-12 educational funding historically originated from the local community, district governing boards have long been empowered with the authority and responsibility to oversee the day-to-day operations of districts. In general, local boards have been able to establish tax rates and generate revenue to provide educational services. Such boards have also been responsible for the hiring and firing of all school personnel, and in most states, for establishing salary levels.

Overall, district governing boards are fairly autonomous, and most decisions are not controversial. Periodically, however, certain constituents (e.g., parent groups, taxpayer groups) believe their views are not being acted upon, especially regarding controversial issues such as school-based clinics, phonics instruction, teacher dismissals, and higher school taxes. These issues have caused conflicts in many communities, leading to the circulation of recall petitions and the development of various factions. Successful school board members have learned to balance the interests of their many constituencies. Some believe this balance makes radical reform virtually impossible.

Most governing board members belong to the National School Boards Association (NSBA) as well as a state affiliate. Being active at both the national and state level, lobbyists for these organizations provide policy information for their members as well as protect their authority. Recently, however, the overall power of district governing boards has diminished due to greater state and federal influences. States' attempts to equalize funding have reduced the freedom of local school boards to levy additional taxes. Consolidation efforts also served to dramatically decrease the numbers of districts, and therefore district governing boards (e.g., in 1938 nearly 120,000 public school districts existed; in

1989, there were slightly more than 15,000). A recent move toward school-site management has led several states (e.g., Kentucky, Illinois) to remove some personnel decisions from the board, while a few states (e.g., Arizona) are considering removing most, if not all, power from the local board. Chapter 3 explores this policy debate.

Officially, district governing boards are considered the primary local policymakers; however, many local boards delegate much of their responsibility to district superintendents (as hired by the board). Depending upon the district's size, several other central office administrators will assist the superintendent in overseeing functions such as budgeting, personnel, research, and curriculum/instruction. Superintendents and their staffs will frequently prepare policy options for board members who in turn "rubber stamp" such recommendations. However, in many large districts, changing board compositions and numerous disparate constituencies have reduced superintendents' tenure (and thus power) considerably.

Far down the chain of command, school-level administrators (e.g., principals) often have only limited authority to establish specific policies for the operation of their schools. In a similar vein, individual teachers have historically had little policy-making authority, although unionized teachers have been extremely influential through collective bargaining agreements. Last of all, students typically have limited impact on policy decisions; however, court cases filed on behalf of students have served to dictate some local policy decisions (e.g., school newspapers and freedom of speech, search and seizure laws).

Teacher Unions

Teachers themselves are a highly educated group; more than 40% hold master's degrees while an additional 7% have education specialist or doctorate degrees. However, unlike other professionals, most belong to a teacher association (union) that collectively bargains over issues such as wages, hours, and working conditions. As the two largest teacher unions, the National Education Association (NEA) has more than 2 million members, or two-thirds of all public school teachers, while the American Federation of Teachers (AFT) has nearly a half-million, or about one-fifth of all public school teachers. NEA members are located in schools throughout the country, while AFT members are located primarily in the big cities of the East and Midwest. NEA's roots can be traced back to the mid-1800s, and historically it has focused on issues of training, curriculum, and instruction; not until the 1960s was NEA considered a union as it began to concentrate on labor/management issues. Quite differently, AFT has focused on more aggressive union activities since its inception during the early 1900s. Collectively, these two groups represent one of the strongest political forces in the United States (Toch, 1991).

The collective power of more than 2.5 million teachers has been put to use at the national, state, and local levels. For example, the NEA became the first education association to organize a national political action committee, which is now one of the largest in the nation. The NEA has been a major supporter of Democratic presidential candidates since 1976, when it played an important role in the Carter campaign. Many view the creation of the U.S. Department of Education under President Jimmy Carter as a sign of appreciation to his backers (Kirst, 1984; Toch, 1991). The NEA and AFT also exert considerable influence in legislative and local school board elections. Well organized and funded, the NEA has extensive national and state networks used to support political candidates in favor of its issues. In most states, these organizations are a strong force that influences the educational policy agenda through lobbying, strikes, and active political support of candidates.

Because of their demands on such blue-collar issues as wages, hours, and working conditions, teacher unions are viewed very negatively by many conservative and moderate policymakers. Through collective bargaining, as backed by their right to strike in some states, many teachers sign annual contracts stipulating conditions such as the minimum hours per day required at school, the maximum number of monthly meetings they must attend, and seniority replacement provisions. Until the early 1980s both the NEA and AFT were strongly opposed to activities such as merit pay and peer review because they maintained that workers should not evaluate each other and that fair representation was needed. These conditions, reflective more of assembly-line workers than professionals, dominated teacher unions for nearly 30 years.

These positions, however, are changing. On the heels of many critical reports released during the early 1980s, Albert Shanker, president of the AFT, became a strong advocate of major educational reforms. Noting that the fruits of collective bargaining—shorter hours, due process protections, a guaranteed salary scale, smaller classes—failed to make teaching a more attractive occupation, Shanker now advocates differentiated teacher salaries, teacher testing, provisions designed to more easily dismiss incompetent teachers, public school choice, alternative certificates, and school restructuring. Most of these reforms are intended to gain more authority for teachers and therefore enhance the profession.

The NEA, on the other hand, remains more committed to the traditional issues of wages, hours, and working conditions. Although many of its members agree with Shanker's move toward restructuring and professionalization, NEA's vast size and decentralized authority structure have made it difficult for the organization to make major philosophical shifts. To that end, NEA continues to block major reform efforts. For example, during the mid-1980s, NEA members boycotted Florida's Master Teacher Plan and took out full-page newspaper advertisements in Miami against a more comprehensive evaluation system (Toch, 1991). Most recently, however, there are signs that NEA members are inching toward many of the reforms being discussed.

In summary, many note that of all nongovernmental groups involved in education, teacher unions have the greatest influence over policymakers (Spring, 1988). Without their support, reforms initiated at the state level may be doomed to failure. Unfortunately, teacher unions are frequently critical of major reforms, especially those not accompanied by increased funding. As a result, many policymakers view them as a roadblock to reform, especially during times of fiscal constraint.

On the other hand, teacher unions represent those who interact daily with students and parents in working conditions that most businesspeople would consider intolerable. Few have phones in their classroom or building, forcing them to wait in line for a single phone in the teachers' lounge. Bells dictate their lives so that a professional lunch is out of the question. Most are still required to perform hall and bus duty, rather than using that time for instructional planning or tutoring students. Although their salaries are decent for a 9-month contract (the average teaching salary during 1990 was $31,304), many seek summer employment to support their families. Teacher unions fought hard during the 1960s and 1970s to get salaries and working conditions to these levels; naturally, they are very reluctant to risk them for something new. Therefore, it is important to remember that many individual teachers are willing to work harder to improve the system, but they have become part of a system that collectively is very cautious about change.

Who Really Controls Education?

In addition to the players identified thus far, dozens of other national, state, and local organizations attempt to influence education policy.

Some focus on the interests of parents and educators, such as the Parent Teachers Association (PTA), American Association of School Administrators (AASA), National Association of Secondary School Principals (NASSP), and Council of Chief State School Officers (CCSSO). Others involve national and state educational research and/or policy groups, such as the Education Commission of the States (ECS), National Council of State Legislators (NCSL), and American Educational Research Association (AERA). Finally, many organizations that have a proprietary interest (e.g., test and textbook companies) have had significant influence over education policy through their lobbyists stationed in Washington, DC, and across the country. In conjunction with the NEA, AFT, and NSBA, these groups have been nicknamed by policymakers the "education alphabets" as they come armed with their proposals for school reform.

Who then controls? In reality, the legal and informal authority of these various groups is not clearly defined; no one entity has primary control over the educational system. Instead, educational governance involves multiple players trying to implement multiple missions. Finn (1991) offers the following image of passing the buck within the current educational system:

> Education, alas, is not so consumer sensitive. Nobody takes responsibility and everyone can get off the hook. The teacher says she is required to use this textbook, isn't allowed to discipline that disruptive youngster, and doesn't have time during the day to provide individual tutoring for the exceptional child. The principal says that the teacher was foisted on him, the textbook decisions are made downtown or by the state, the school board will not allot funds for tutors, and the courts have tied his hands with respect to discipline. The superintendent explains that the principal has tenure (and besides, his wife's cousin is an alderman); the school board is adamant that handicapped and disadvantaged children receive all the tutorial help, even if it leaves none for gifted youngsters. The board chairman says he is following the superintendent's professional advice, and in any case, is constrained by state and federal law. The governor observes that the schools in this state are locally controlled and the teacher's union and school board association helped elect him. The congressman sends back a polite form letter indicating that your views will be carefully considered the next time pertinent legislation comes before the House. From the federal Department of Education, there is no reply for six months; then you receive a pamphlet entitled "How to Help Your Child Improve in Math." (p. 184)

This does not paint a pretty picture of who really controls education and who is thus responsible. However, it is a realistic portrayal of political dynamics within the educational arena. In an attempt to minimize centralized power, a very fragmented system of control has evolved, easily impacted by powerful constituencies. Although each group represents people who have the interests of children at heart, seldom do these groups form a common agenda. Instead, they have become friendly rivals supporting each other in public, yet vying for limited resources behind closed doors. Some contend that the internal dynamics and rivalries of the educational system have frequently pushed aside the public interest and well-being of students. On the other hand, our society has never come to terms with what the educational system is to accomplish, thus allowing various values to compete.

Overall, our decentralized education system has served to maximize local liberties, but at the expense of equity, efficiency, and excellence. Indeed, multiple lines of control have led to great resource and outcome disparities, which in turn have generated considerable controversy. One underlying consideration is money. Each interest group, wanting to ensure funding for its agenda, must scramble to acquire resources from a finite pool. Several questions arise: How much fiscal equity exists in the current system, what impact have the courts had in this debate, and does additional money translate into increased educational excellence and efficiency? These issues are investigated in the next section as well as in subsequent chapters.

School Financing—The Great Equity Debate

If asked what single educational policy topic drives key debates, most policymakers would note the financing of education. Faced daily with demands for additional resources, many legislators have suffered through lawsuits challenging the inequities of their state's school financing system. School finance debates involve value conflicts that pit conservatives and liberals against each other as few other topics can. Liberals believe additional resources are necessary for excellence, while conservatives contend that increased revenues are unwarranted because schooling can become more efficient. Conflict abounds.

How Equal Are We?

Large differences exist in per-student spending both between and within states. For example, in 1989-1990, New Jersey spent an average of $8,439 per student, more than three times as much as the $2,720 per student spent in Utah, the lowest-spending state. A criticism to inferences based on these data is the great variation in state costs of living. To that end, Figure 2.2 illustrates the average expenditure per pupil after adjustment for cost of living. Although disparities are narrowed somewhat, a range of nearly $7,000 in New York to slightly less than $3,000 in Utah is evident, making the expenditures of the highest-spending state more than double that of the lowest.

Differences within states are also significant and serve as primary evidence in school finance court cases. These disparities occur because most districts are allowed to generate local funds *in addition* to the minimum level that the state provides. In some cases, these additional local revenues are limited (e.g., a maximum of 15% in Arizona with voter approval); however, most states do not cap the amount that can be generated through a local election approval process. Consequently, great inequities exist. A recent study determined that in 12 states, some school districts were spending at least twice as much per student than others; in New York, the difference between the top districts and the bottom districts was more than $6,000—more than most states provide in total per pupil on education (Barton, Coley, & Goertz, 1991). Although debate continues, few can argue that districts with less than half the annual revenue of other districts will be able to offer the same educational opportunities, especially for expensive instructional programming such as technology.

For example, in Montana, recent studies showed that wealthy districts had a ratio of 13 students per teacher, compared to ratios in the high 20s and 30s within poor districts. In addition, poor districts were found to have substandard facilities, outdated equipment and textbooks, and fewer offerings in English and music. Using these data, the Montana courts in 1989 declared the state's school finance system unconstitutional. In Kentucky, the state Supreme Court found that poorer districts had lower teacher salaries and less adequate programs in mathematics, science, foreign language, music, and art. This state's system was also declared unconstitutional in 1989.

Similar examples of inequity can be extracted from most states; however, court challenges in Oklahoma, North Carolina, Louisiana, and

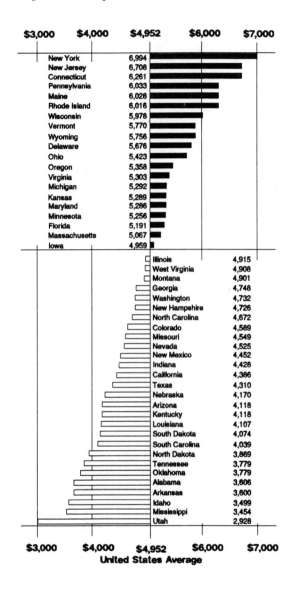

Figure 2.2. Average Expenditure per Pupil Adjusted for Cost-of-Living, 1989-1990

SOURCE: *The State of Inequality* by P. E. Barton, R. J. Coley, & M. E. Goertz, 1991, p. 5. Princeton, NJ: Policy Information Center, Educational Testing Services. Reprinted with permission.
NOTE: Adjusted expenditures not available for Alaska and Hawaii due to factors involving climate and transportation.

South Carolina during 1987 and 1988 found such disparities did not render their school finance systems unconstitutional. How can this be? Since each ruling depends upon the state's specific constitutional provisions and the data and arguments offered by the plaintiffs, various interpretations will occur. A brief history of school finance litigation and the ongoing debate follows.

Impact of the Courts

From the inception of the American educational system until the late 1970s, local property wealth was the primary source of funding for most school districts. Initially, legislators were reluctant to accept responsibility for imposing taxes at the state level, and therefore delegated substantial taxing authorities to localities. As a result, the amount of funding available per pupil was (and still is) directly related to the property wealth of the district and the willingness of the residents to tax themselves for education. Districts with high property wealth have substantially more resources than districts with low property wealth; the combined economic circumstances of a community's families thus determine the school's resources. Inequities in funding were initially accepted with little debate because Americans had become accustomed to local control. Therefore, people did not publicly question whether inequitable funding systems denied students equal educational opportunities until several studies in the mid-1960s revealed great disparities in educational achievement and resources.

The first wave of school finance court cases began in the late 1960s. Most utilized the equal protection clause of the Fourteenth Amendment to challenge states' methods of distributing funds, claiming that children in property-poor school districts were being discriminated against. These initial cases were unsuccessful in their challenges until, in 1971, the California Supreme Court ruled in *Serrano v. Priest* that the unequal distribution of funds did violate the equal protection clauses of both the U.S. and California constitutions. It appeared that the door had been opened to declaring education a fundamental right worthy of equal protection. In 1973, however, the U.S. Supreme Court quickly closed this door in *San Antonio Independent School District v. Rodriguez,* holding that disparate allocation of state tax resources did not violate the equal protection clause of the U.S. Constitution. As a result, school financing cases are now being decided on protections offered within state constitutions, which vary greatly across the country.

From 1971 through 1983, court challenges were filed in 19 states. Ten of these state courts declared their school finance formula constitutional; in nine, the formula was declared unconstitutional (Alexander, 1991). Prodded by actual or threatened lawsuits, many states enacted new or revised education "equalization" formulae whereby additional state funding was provided to low property wealth districts. States also began to provide program funding for special education and limited English proficient pupils. Although some equity gains were made by raising the level of low-spending districts, few caps were placed on the high-spending districts. Vast disparities continued.

The next round of school finance cases began to appear during the late 1980s, with plaintiffs now focusing on language within the "education provisions" of their state constitutions rather than on the equal protection clause. These provisions were frequently crafted to reflect the spirit of the common school ideal—that public schools are to be free and equal. For example, Kentucky's constitution requires "an efficient system of common schools"; Texas' constitution requires "an efficient system of public free schools"; while Arizona's constitution requires "such laws as shall provide for the establishment and maintenance of a general and uniform public school system" (Alexander, 1991, p. 353). Using this line of reasoning, plaintiffs began to win cases against the state, including recent cases in Montana (1989), Kentucky (1989), Texas (1989), New Jersey (1990), and Tennessee (1991).

The courts also began to play a stronger role in educational policy-making. Prior to this time, legislative control over education had been considered to be plenary, limited only by the individual rights and freedoms as stated in the federal or state constitutions. However, the Kentucky Supreme Court declared unconstitutional the state's entire system of common schools, not just the finance system. It ruled that reasons for the vast differences in per pupil resources within the state were deficient in constitutional rationale and justification. The court's action led to a complete revision of school financing and substantial modification in the organization and administration of Kentucky's public schools. New tax legislation brought in nearly $1 billion for the state's first biannual budget following legislative adoption of the new educational provisions. These reforms and their impact are detailed in other chapters of this book, but a key point is that financial equity, as well as quality of educational programming, has been substantially influenced by the courts in Kentucky. Many believe that other state courts will follow this lead.

Why is the provision of fiscal equity so difficult to accomplish? Theoretically, it is simple to devise an equitable school financing system. The state would set a uniform state tax for education, collect that amount from every taxpayer, and then redistribute the funds on an equalized per pupil amount. No additional local revenues would be allowed, and all taxpayers would pay the same tax rate. Any disparities among per pupil expenditures could be explained by differences in student needs (e.g., special education), not property wealth. Although the resulting financing system would be a bit more complex than portrayed above, the concepts are still fairly simple. Why has this not occurred?

First, tax revenues from high property wealth districts would be recaptured for use in low property wealth districts: that is, take from the rich and give to the poor. Current high-spending districts would probably be forced to spend less as the state brought districts to an average level. Community members would not be allowed to generate additional revenues through local school financing elections, hence lowering their "right" to local control. In addition, the representative nature of the legislature is sufficient to prevent the above scenario. Because legislators have been elected to represent the interests of their constituents, self-interest frequently prevails over the common good. Finally, some contend that the public is less likely to support statewide funding, and not enough is known about the true costs of education to set one funding level for every district.

Although school finance litigation continues (in 1991, it was occurring in at least 21 states), the notion of allowable inequities based upon local taxpayers' choice to supplement state revenues remains. This reflects the ideology that taxpayers should be able to voice opinions regarding the excellence of their school district by saying "yes" or "no" to additional taxes. As a result, major conflicts between local liberties and government's need to equalize resources exist; debates surrounding school finance equity will continue for the foreseeable future.

Adequacy Debates—Does Money Make a Difference?

One ongoing debate concerns whether additional resources make a difference in student outcomes and excellence. A common scenario at legislative hearings across the country involves a group of educators and parents testifying about the needs of their school, offering a host of statistics illustrating increased poverty rates and child abuse. In response, conservatives call for elimination of bureaucratic waste and cite statistics showing large increases in educational spending during the 1980s, with few tangible outcomes. Unfortunately, neither group convinces the other, and the debate continues. A quick glance at the research is in order.

As one of the first highly publicized reports on this topic, James Coleman's *Equality of Educational Opportunity Report* (1965) found that student achievement did not vary across schools in close relation to available resources after controlling for socioeconomic factors (Educational Testing Service, 1991). The implication was that increasing school inputs did not reliably lead to stronger education outcomes. Although this finding did not draw much attention in 1965, it is now cited, along with similar findings, by those who oppose large infusions of money to improve the educational system. Finn (1991) contends that federal officials who sensed its power actually hid the original Coleman finding within a large technical report.

In 1989 Eric Hanushek summarized the outcomes of 187 relevant studies and, in agreement with the Coleman Report, concluded that strong and consistent evidence exists to show expenditures are not systematically related to student achievement. He notes that the emphasis on expenditure differences in school finance court cases or legislative deliberations is misguided, given the evidence.

Others, such as Smith and O'Day (1991), offer a different view of these same studies. They agree that these data show few educational outcome gains, but highlight the studies' many methodological flaws. First, it is difficult to separate the effects of variations in school finances from the effect of what money buys. High-quality teachers may opt for lower salaries in districts that have the money to support superior working conditions. A second argument is that few studies have adequately controlled for the cost of purchasing services. Relatively high per pupil expenditures in a major city may not purchase the same level of resources as smaller amounts in a less costly setting. Smith and O'Day conclude, "In our society it is impossible to argue that, other things such as purchasing power being roughly equal, major disparities in finances, especially those that favor the most advantaged in society, will not impede EEO [equal educational opportunity]" (p. 66).

In reviewing this statistical debate, researchers from Educational Testing Service (1991) generally agree with Smith and O'Day. They note that in many studies, it is difficult to determine the effects of expenditure levels due to the high intercorrelation of spending with socioeconomic factors. In addition, since data gathered in these studies are largely gross measures, such as total expenditures per pupil or years of education of teachers, the studies have not probed specific classroom factors that affect learning. For example, using data from the 1990 NAEP mathematics assessment, these researchers report a link between the instructional resources that teachers have available to them and the mathematics proficiency of their students. Average mathematics scores were lower in classrooms where teachers had fewer resources. However, in examining these same data using gross expenditures per students, there was little relationship to average mathematics proficiency.

As discussed above, there is plenty of room for debate within the statistical "facts." One view finds no systematic relationship and argues that more equitable or larger distribution of resources will do little to advance educational excellence. The other side believes that addressing inequity and adequacy are keys to improving education. No clear answer regarding the relationship between resources and educational achievement exists.

The newly adopted national goals as stated in President Bush's *America 2000* plan, and subsequent efforts to achieve those goals, are adding fuel to the fiscal equity debates. How do substantial funding disparities both across and within states affect the goal of having all children in the nation accomplish similar minimum outcomes by the year 2000? How will parental choice programs affect local taxing plans since many students will no longer be enrolled in their resident districts? Driven by local control over funding, multiple constituencies, and conflicting research results, debates on school financing will continue to rage in the courtroom and in legislative hearing rooms.

As a point of departure, the following quote is an appropriate commentary on education finance equity debates: "School finance reform is like a 19th-century Russian novel. The story line runs across generations, the plot is complex, the prose is tedious, and everybody dies in the end" (State Policy Research, Inc., 1992).

In Summary

To provide a foundation for reviewing current controversial education policy debates, Chapters 1 and 2 have presented diverse information regarding the American educational system. Underlying values of equity, efficiency, liberty, and excellence were introduced and will be tracked throughout the book. A brief historical sketch of the ever-evolving system illustrates the cycles of reform that place the current debates in context. Contrasting education to the private sector illustrates many organizational and cultural differences. The cursory review of the many entities that attempt to control educational policy-making depicts a system where, in effect, no one is in charge, but plurality flourishes. Finally, a glance at the financing of our system reveals vast disparities and ongoing court battles. Using these issues as a backdrop, a more careful review of key education policy issues and debates follows.

3

———— ■ ————

What's Wrong With the Way the Educational System Is Organized?

Introduction

If you were to walk into a typical American classroom today, it would look much like it did when you, your parents, or even your grandparents went to school. Despite such differences as a computer or two in the back, students using calculators, desks clustered in small groups, and, of course, clothes and hairstyles, the fundamental structure of the school has changed little. The teacher typically lectures from the front of the classroom on a single subject area, students take notes and complete exercises from the textbook or worksheets, bells ring or a certain amount of time passes, and students move from subject to subject. The day is broken into discrete activities seldom integrated, especially at the secondary level.

The school year is also similar. Students are released for 3 months in the summer—continuing a tradition from when children were needed to help gather the crops. High school teachers are responsible for educating and grading assignments for 150 different students each day. Elementary teachers are responsible for approximately 25 students, but they must prepare lessons for six to eight different subjects a day. Bells, lectures, learning fragmented into subject areas, the first 6 weeks each year spent reteaching what was forgotten over the summer, isolated teaching conditions, and extensive use of textbooks are key features of schooling that have changed little over time. Few aspects of our society have remained so untouched.

Control of the schools also looks the same. A locally elected governing board meets monthly to discuss policy decisions such as the lunch program or the yearly district calendar. District office personnel develop standardized curriculum models to meet state guidelines. Vocal parents insist that their children be assigned to certain teachers and claim that the principal or teachers are not responsive enough to their needs. Legislators and state board members hold hearings and develop policies in reaction to the latest crisis at hand, but seldom as part of a larger state plan.

This is not to say that experimentation within our K-12 educational system has not occurred. Open classrooms, new math, cooperative learning, peer tutoring, computer-assisted instruction, team teaching, year-round schooling, site-based management, writing across the curriculum, and strategic plans represent past and current attempts to reform the school structure and instruction. A few reforms left residue (e.g., instructional aides); some have just begun (e.g., educational warranties); others are back for the second cycle (e.g., year-round schooling).

Underneath these reform efforts, however, lies a system that looks a great deal like an assembly line. Students enter school at a certain age, and promotion from grade to grade is more dependent upon chronological progression than upon acquisition of knowledge or attainment of skills. During the day, teachers "pour" a little bit of math, a section of science, a dose of English, and a portion of foreign language into students' minds. During the life of a student, the assembly line keeps moving, with teachers plugging in skills that have been labeled as 3rd, 7th, or 10th grade skills. Over time, society has required more complex products—students knowing the basics as well as fine arts and vocational education—and in response, several tracks have been created. As with any assembly line, some products are defective due to an earlier part that did not quite fit correctly or raw material with quality defects. These products are removed from the line (i.e., dropouts), or continue to the end to be shipped off, even though they do not function properly. As Kearns and Doyle (1988) note:

Most of our schools look a lot like factories, and almost without exception, have the gray personality of a government bureaucracy. Working conditions are uniform—uniformly drab and difficult. Salaries are on a fixed schedule that bears little or no relationship to accomplishment. Internal and external incentives and rewards are few and far between. There is little opportunity for true collegiality and disciplinary development, as there is in colleges, universities, and private R&D settings. The physical plant is frequently inadequate to the task expected of the teacher. Rare is the teacher with his own office, or even a regular place to work away from the students, or to make or receive a phone call in private. Professionals in other walks of life would find that incomprehensible and unacceptable. (p. 52)

One reflex is to blame the educational system for doing such a disparaging job. What most critics do not realize, however, is that our educational system was intentionally crafted to look this way. While our forefathers did not set out to design a system in which only a certain number of students would succeed, the structure of American schooling was driven by the goal to educate the masses, including an ever-growing number of immigrants. It gathered input from scientific management principles during the 1930s, the same strategies used to sharpen industrial processes in factories during that time. It was also driven by an American public that expected schools not only to educate their children, but also to solve all of society's ills. Finally, to minimize the threat of centralized control, a very decentralized state, rather than national, system was created. It was not one master plot, but instead a strategy that evolved to educate a burgeoning population, using teachers who resemble blue-collar laborers more than professionals. Much like American industries, schools are now being forced to change toward a high-tech model. As Albert Shanker (1990), president of the American Federation of Teachers, writes:

When the factory was touted as the ideal organization for work and when most youngsters were headed for its assembly lines, making a mass public education system conform to the model of a factory may have seemed like a great achievement. When we were content to educate a small percentage of our students and flunk the others or let them drop out, the limitations of that model were not much apparent and did not seem serious. But America's old-fashioned factories are dead or dying and will not be resurrected as we know them. . . . The limitations of America's traditional factory model of education have become manifest, and they are crippling. (p. 350)

Unfortunately, controversy over the quality of schooling comes from a lack of understanding on all sides—those within the system are tired of being put down by those on the outside and are resistant to change, while those on the outside continue to push their ideas with little knowledge of issues and with little respect for those within. This relationship has improved recently, but not quickly enough and not in every state.

This chapter briefly examines the evolution of our educational structure, expanding on the historical sketch provided in Chapter 1. It also examines many of the issues related to "restructuring" that are being debated and attempted across the country. As in other chapters of this book, readers are not left with concrete answers, but instead are provided with thoughts to further the intellectual debate.

Restructuring Defined

Several terms will be used throughout this chapter. *Restructuring* is a global term that implies a radical redesign of the current educational system. This involves more than simply improving or reforming the system, but examining each component—curriculum, roles of teachers and staff, teaching and learning strategies, governance, financing, accountability, community support—and reconstructing as necessary to meet the needs of all students. Although frequently used in a synonymous manner, *reform* generally implies improving the current system rather than making fundamental changes.

Viewed as one element of restructuring, *decentralization* involves the transfer of decision-making authority and responsibility from a more centralized entity to those implementing the decisions. Decentralization can mean a shifting of authority from the state board of education to the local district governing board and/or from the local governing board/central office to the local school. As a subset of decentralization, *school-based management* or *school-site decision making* implies giving school personnel the authority to operate their school. Within school-based management, redistribution of authority typically occurs in any or all of three areas: budget, curriculum, and personnel.

Overall, restructuring has been a key buzzword of educational policy debates since the late 1980s. However, although many educational

systems have implemented improvements or reforms during the past
decade, few, if any, have resulted in major restructuring.

The Rise of Centralization
and the "Educational Bureaucracy"

As advocated by Mann and others during the 1830s, the common
school was to include children from all classes, sects, and ethnic groups,
and it was to serve a general purpose—to give pupils a basic elementary
education that would equip them for participation in a democracy and
entrance into the world of work. Egalitarianism was an underlying
principle in that all citizens should have equal rights and opportunities;
for this to occur, education was necessary. Many individual schools
were built and supervised by lay people, while young, mostly untrained
teachers instructed the pupils. In large cities, numerous local boards and
committees oversaw the schools. Decentralization was at its peak during the mid-1800s because virtually no state or central office educational bureaucracies existed.

By the turn of the century (1890-1910) however, local control had
run amok, as evidenced by municipal corruption in the city offices as
well as in the educational system. Kirst (1984) notes that in 1905,
Philadelphia had 43 elected school boards with 559 members while the
Cincinnati school board had 74 subcommittees; control by the people
was the norm. He writes:

> Muckrakers exposed textbook publishers and contractors who allied them-
> selves with corrupt school trustees for common boodle in the common
> school. . . . This situation was reinforced with a vengeance by local con-
> trol. A ward-based, decentralized committee system for administering the
> public schools provided opportunities for extensive political influence.
> (p. 31-32)

Business and professional leaders contended that ward elections for
board members advanced special interests at the expense of the school
board as a whole. In addition, extensive use of subcommittees led to
inefficiencies. It was believed that better management could occur by
centralizing power in a chief executive. Attempts were made to remove
local politics from the educational system by consolidating smaller

schools into larger township or regional districts, with centralized boards composed mainly of professional businessmen. Wirt and Kirst (1989) note that the key reform principles during this time were efficiency, expertise, professionalism, centralization, and nonpolitical control.

At the same time, emerging large industrial corporate bureaucracies became an attractive model for school reform as part of the "scientific management" movement. In an attempt to increase efficiency, a fine-tuning of work procedures was incorporated into many factory settings. The same thinking behind the mass production of cars was applied to the mass education of students. Because of the increased number of students enrolling in the public schools due to child labor laws and continued immigration, many believed that such efficiencies were necessary.

The impact of the scientific movement was to establish "teacher-proof" schools through centralized decision making, inflexible work rules and schedules, and standardized curriculum. For the sake of efficiency, the following was created:

> One best system in which all the nation's schools would run as one: The curriculum would drive the schools. Administration, management, organization, rules of work, and behavior would look almost like the modern factory. . . . The taxpayers are the shareholders; the school board, the board of trustees; the superintendent, the C.E.O.; the deputy superintendent, the division manager; the principal, the foremen; the teachers, the workers on the assembly line. The product is students, turned out with the same attention to quality control the factory paid to its product. (Doyle, 1989, p. 27)

The move toward efficiency had great success. In 1929 there were nearly 120,000 school districts with 240,000 elementary schools (of which 150,000 were one-teacher schools). By 1955 the number of districts had been reduced by more than two-thirds (to 55,000) while the number of elementary schools decreased by more than one-half (to 104,000). As originally crafted by the move to centralization, weak links existed between the community patrons and the school administrators.

Also during this time, teachers began to grow in both power and number (from just more than one million in 1940 to almost 2.5 million in 1971). Partly as a result of centralization, teachers found themselves distanced from the school board and the public. Once viewed as submissive, they began to form unions, to engage in collective bargaining, and to strike. They also became involved in both state and federal politics. Following the tradition of the nation's industrial labor unions, teachers began demanding the right to bargain for wages, hours, and working conditions. By 1974 more than 60% of the nation's 2 million teachers were working under collective bargaining agreements; just a few years later, nearly 90% were members of either the American Federation of Teachers (AFT) or the National Education Association (NEA), making public school teaching the most highly unionized occupation in the nation (Toch, 1991). Unfortunately, too much focus was spent on labor versus management conflicts, rather than on improving teaching and learning. Instead of serving to break down centralization, the union created its own layer of teacher bureaucracy.

During the 1960s and 1970s equity for all students—minorities, females, handicapped, limited English proficient, and the poor—led to major increases in federal funding. In addition, the teacher unions lobbied for additional federal resources and programs. These activities led to growth in national, state, and local education bureaucracies due to compliance requirements of such programs. Because the resulting regulations had become so restrictive, this focus on equity served to decrease local programming options and system efficiencies.

In an attempt to break down growing bureaucracies, a wave of decentralization occurred within most big city school districts during the 1960s and 1970s (Guthrie, Garms, & Pierce, 1988). Many districts were divided into administrative units, each with an executive officer in charge of all subdistrict schools. In New York City, for example, election of subdistrict boards was initiated. The amount of authority granted to these boards over financing, curriculum, and personnel varied greatly, but much remained a central office function. Most contend that little was accomplished through this decentralization, except to add additional bureaucratic layers between the schools and the real decision-makers.

The 1980s saw the first phase of the current educational reform movement. Interestingly, it also saw the continued increase in centralization and state oversight. Reforms such as student and teacher testing, state standards, increased credits for graduation, no pass/no play, and even parental choice, led to greater state and local oversight (Timar, 1989). Governors and legislators became leaders in the educational reform agenda, and many of the reform initiatives were mandated from the state level with little regard for diverse local school contexts. Indeed, some of these reforms failed within a few years, while others remained to add little but paperwork. Ironically, education was perhaps more regulated and centralized during the late 1980s than ever before in our country's history. Calls to reverse this trend came loudly and quickly.

A New Awareness

As already noted, decentralization of schooling was the norm at the turn of the century, yet political corruption and inefficiency forced business leaders and professionals to implement changes. In response, centrally planned, mass production schooling was developed to capitalize upon efficiency principles. Indeed, it had been the model for most of American industry and, at least prior to World War II, had worked reasonably well.

The country's focus on equal educational opportunities during the 1960s and 1970s produced greater equity for students, as well as large administrative staffs to oversee such programs. State legislators and corporate leaders urged a much stronger state role in accountability and standards during the 1980s, resulting in top-down mandates and additional management layers. These activities resulted in some centralized efficiency, greater student equity, but little excellence. Not surprisingly, these same policymakers and reform advocates are now attempting to lead schools back toward decentralization. Just as labor unions, assembly lines, and layers of management served to cripple the American auto industry, it is believed that the same has occurred in education.

Unfortunately, many continue to blame those within the system for its current deficiencies, rather than realizing the system is working quite well in accomplishing what it was intended to do—educate the masses for a relatively small amount per unit. Many conservatives contend that additional money poured into an industrial model of schooling serves little purpose. They believe it is time to stop tinkering with the system and create one that will meet the needs of present and future students. America must go beyond upgrading a school system designed for an agricultural society of the nineteenth century, to a more fundamental approach of rebuilding a school system prepared for the twenty-first century. In contrast, most liberals believe the overall system is fine but that additional resources are needed to meet society's increasing demands. Others acknowledge that our industrial model has reached its limit, but agree that additional resources are essential. Shanker (1990) notes: "Given our present and foreseeable demographic, economic, social, and educational circumstances, we can expect neither great efficiency nor more equity from our [current] education system" (p. 345).

In sum, reform leaders of the 1990s are calling for a complete restructuring of the educational system. For example, the National Alliance of Business (1990) recommends that seven key areas of restructuring are necessary to fundamentally change the way schools, districts, and state agencies are run and do business:

1. Revamping organization, management, and administration;
2. Developing the professionalism of teachers and administrators;
3. Redesigning or updating curriculum and instruction methods;
4. Instituting accountability and performance standards;
5. Integrating and linking community and social service delivery;
6. Developing effective and efficient systems for financing and budgeting education; and
7. Upgrading the quality of the educational infrastructure.

What Does a Restructured System Look Like?

Since restructuring involves fundamental changes in a vast education enterprise, many different approaches are being utilized across the country. Some of the more common themes involve the implementation of school-site councils (e.g., Kentucky, Chicago, Los Angeles); the revamping of state departments of education to become less regulatory and more of a support center (e.g., Kentucky, Virginia); the granting of state waivers from rules and regulations (more than a dozen states); the creation of new curricula frameworks linked to performance-based assessments (e.g., Arizona, California, Vermont); and additional funding to schools wishing to pilot restructuring activities such as nongraded schools, site-based management, and year-round schooling (e.g., Washington, Texas). Other recent approaches involve subcontracting with private for-profit firms to manage the school districts, such as in Duluth, Minnesota; or in the case of Chelsea, Massachusetts, the public school district is being run by a team from Boston University. Finally, a great deal of private corporate and/or foundation funding is being deployed to develop "break-the-mold" schools (e.g., New American Schools Development Corporation).

Prior to discussing debates surrounding these issues, several existing American and international educational entities that have begun the restructuring process will be profiled. Reviewing these systems will illustrate vast differences from current norms.

Cologne, Germany

The Holweide Comprehensive School in Cologne is not the typical German school by any means; instead, it represents an experiment initiated during the late 1970s. Within this school of about 2,200 students, teachers work in teams of six to eight members and are responsible for the education of 90 to 120 students for 6 years of schooling (grades 5 through 10). The team of teachers decides how to group students and organize the day, and who will teach specific subjects and serve on school-wide committees. Student groups are formed of mixed abilities and ages for every subject; peer support and tutoring are the norm. Students work together on problems, where questions take precedence over teacher lectures. Since a group of students remains with the same teachers for 6 years, continuous and cooperative learning can occur—no instructional time is lost becoming familiar with the students' names, skills, and needs. In addition, the teachers can blame no one else for student deficiencies; working as a team, they must assume responsibility for the graduation of each student.

Holweide's minimal school administration consists of one principal and two assistants who also teach part-time. In addition, a governing panel of senior teachers, primarily elected by fellow teachers, assists in the oversight of the school. Parents offer a variety of extracurricular classes (e.g., music, sports) during the lunch period, thereby lessening the load of the teachers and exposing students to more activities (Ratzki & Fisher, 1990). These authors also note positive program outcomes in that less than 1% of the students in the school drop out, and about 60% score well enough to be admitted to the 3-year college that leads to the university (the overall German average is 37%). This school has been the subject of keen interest to reform experts, and several similar models have been developed in the United States.

Kentucky's Education Reform Act of 1990

Implementing a state-wide model of reform, Kentucky has recently undertaken many comprehensive changes. Driven by a State Supreme Court decision that declared the entire system of K-12 schooling unconstitutional, Kentucky had a rare opportunity to enact sweeping changes. In addition to a complete revamping of its financing system, it has initiated restructuring of governance, accountability, and instruction across the state. As extracted from a summary prepared by Miller, Noland, and Schaaf (1990), key changes in reference to governance and accountability include:

- School councils have been formed for site-based decision making.
- The power to hire and fire school personnel, except for the school district superintendent, has been removed from local school boards.
- The state department of education was restructured to abolish all positions, terminating all employees at the end of fiscal year 1990-1991. Many existing employees were rehired into new or existing positions; however, some were not. The department has also reorganized to create regional service centers.
- All powers have been removed from the previously elected Superintendent of Public Instruction, and a new State Board for Elementary and Secondary Education was appointed by the governor. This board now hires a Commissioner of Education to oversee the state system.
- An Office of Education Accountability has been created as an independent arm of the legislature in order to monitor the outcomes of the educational system.
- A comprehensive "rewards and sanctions" system is being developed for both district and school levels.

Key changes in instructional practices and social service support include:

- An ungraded "primary school program" is being created to replace the previous Grades 1 through 3.
- Curriculum frameworks and performance-based assessments that match these frameworks are being developed (i.e., an alignment between what is taught and what is tested).
- Schools are receiving additional funding to provide extended days, weeks, or years for students requiring additional support.

- Developmentally appropriate half-day preschools are being initiated for all at-risk 4-year-olds.
- A network of family and youth resource centers is being created to support the nonschool needs of students and families.
- A long-range technology plan, including everything from telephones in every classroom to a statewide fiber-optic system, is being developed.

Although these represent just a sample of the reforms currently being implemented in every Kentucky public school, they permit the reader to grasp the comprehensive nature of these changes. However, some believe that many of these activities are more reforms than restructuring and that too much was mandated top-down from the state. Nonetheless, considering that Kentucky's educational system had been one of the worst in the country prior to these changes, and the necessary energy and willpower to make statewide changes, these reform activities are indeed remarkable. Understandably, the state continues to have major reform/restructuring "pains" as financial resources become finite and actual implementation occurs.

Arizona's Task Force on Educational Reform

Initiated by Governor Fife Symington during 1991, this broad-based task force recommended a radical decentralization plan as part of its reform package. Under this plan, essentially all power would be given to individual schools rather than to the local district governing board. Using a town-hall-style forum, school communities would develop decision-making units to decide how much authority and responsibility they want. For example, a school might choose to take on curriculum and personnel decisions, but contract with its central office (or some other public or private entity) for transportation, maintenance, and bookkeeping. As a result, local district boards and central offices would maintain only those powers granted them by their schools. Elements of this concept have been advocated by others such as Chubb and Moe (1990) and Shanker (1990).

Whereas choice used to be the most controversial issue in Arizona, decentralization debates have now become paramount. Critics are able to pick apart the logistics of this decentralization plan very quickly. For example, who remains the legal entity in lawsuits—the school or district? If the local board no longer has control over budgeting, and the local school decision-making units are not elected, is there a problem of taxation without representation? Teacher associations are concerned with having to negotiate with more than 1,000 school units rather than 200-plus local governing boards. District governing boards and superintendents are concerned with legal issues and inefficiencies. Many are wondering if this is just another educational reform fad that will also pass. During spring 1992 the Arizona legislature debated this concept as well as other comprehensive reform bills (e.g., choice, accountability). Given both the radical nature of the decentralization proposal and the strong opposing forces, the proposed reforms were modified significantly, and ultimately defeated.

The Holweide school in Germany, and the states of Kentucky and Arizona, are just three of many entities that have undertaken (or are considering) major reform and restructuring efforts. For example, since 1988, Great Britain's local education authorities (the equivalent of American school districts) must give school personnel complete control over 85% of the school's budget. In addition, schools that want complete autonomy can opt out of their local education authority altogether, receiving money and guidance from only the national government (Chira, 1992). Other U.S. districts commonly profiled as undergoing comprehensive restructuring efforts include Rochester, New York; Chicago, Illinois; and Dade County, Florida. Other states include Arkansas, South Carolina, Vermont, and Minnesota, while specific national programs include Ted Sizer's *Re: Learning* project and Henry Levin's *Accelerated Schools*. A National Governors' Association study on restructuring efforts indicates that every state can point to exciting new ventures, but most of what is called restructuring reflects improvement in only a fraction of the system. In addition, most activities are limited to pilot projects rather than systematic statewide application.

Why the Debate?

After reviewing these examples, it should be evident why this topic is controversial. There is little question of the need to restructure, but instead debates focus on "how" and "how radical." Some reformers say the system is so entrenched that only strong competition and market forces (i.e., choice) will drive real change (Doyle, 1989; Finn, 1991). Little additional money is needed since implementation of public and private school choice and deregulation will encourage needed changes (i.e., create greater efficiencies). Others, including many educators, readily admit that the system needs a complete overhaul, but that time and resources are necessary to prepare educators for the changes ahead. Also, within these excellence "experiments," some students could get hurt. William Kolberg, president of the National Alliance of Business, writes: "Restructuring is never comfortable. Just ask any businessperson who has undergone the upheaval. Restructuring is a risky and costly venture, fraught with difficulty. But schools, like successful businesses, must see change as an opportunity, not a threat" (National Alliance of Business, 1989, p. iii).

It Takes Time, Training, and Money

Marc Tucker (1991), of the National Center on Education and the Economy, notes that lessons from corporate America show restructuring takes time and funding. Using Motorola as an example, Tucker notes that the company has been working on the concept for more than 11 years, and its training budget has increased from $7 million per year to $120 million. As part of the process, the company realized it had to make basic changes in goals, investment patterns, management strategies, incentive structures, hiring practices, teaching methods, and its overall corporate culture, and to that end, has not yet reached its goal. "The great firms would surely have taken a shorter, less demanding route to quality and excellence if one were available. But none exists" (Tucker, 1991, p. 62).

Those attempting to implement restructuring activities within their districts and schools note it is difficult for teachers, who currently dedicate most of their day to instructional responsibilities, to find time for site-based management team meetings. In addition, time is required to learn the background and details of an issue so that appropriate decisions can be made. Few teachers (and even principals) understand how school finance and budgeting work. Nor are they familiar with state laws and regulations related to curriculum, personnel, building codes, and bidding procedures, or federal and state laws focused on special education, bilingual education, and desegregation. These are just a fraction of the issues for which teachers, principals, and parents might become accountable when taking on decision-making responsibilities. Just as many organizations have found that time and resources are needed to create a new corporate culture, many believe it will take at least as much for a new "educational culture."

On the other hand, many educational reform advocates are impatient and want change now. After having invested a large amount of new money during the 1980s, while seeing little gain in test scores, many policymakers are leery of making additional investments. Finn (1991) indicates that the average salary paid to U.S. public school teachers rose 27% during the 1980s after adjustment for inflation, while increases for other professions were much lower (e.g., 14% for engineers; 18% for attorneys). Using an annualized figure for a 48-week year, the average public school teacher would have earned approximately $44,400 in 1990-1991. Some believe that teachers are adequately paid for 9 contract months and that any additional salaries should buy additional teacher time. Teachers may also find additional time if the tradeoff is greater decision-making control over their school and profession.

Many contend that education far underspends on training and staff development when compared with private business. For example, education spends less than 1% on employee training, compared to 5% to 7% within large corporate settings. However, others point out that these figures for education do not include either the money spent on salary increases for additional university credits earned or the state funding used to underwrite such courses. The vast majority of teachers receive raises after they attain post-baccalaureate university credits or attend workshops. Although district approval is necessary, most courses or workshops offered by Colleges of Education are acceptable. As a result, teachers spend a large portion of their summers and evenings taking graduate-level courses that are frequently a "disorganized patchwork of often irrelevant workshops, lectures, and college courses. . . . [such requirements] have spawned a billion-dollar-a-year industry for education schools, a myriad of consulting firms, and others, who vie to give teachers the most credits for the least amount of work" (Toch, 1991, p. 199). If the reward system were restructured to focus on performance rather than years of experience and educational credits earned, some believe that portions of current salary dollars could be used for planning and focused training. This is easier said than done, but some schools and districts have tackled this idea.

As noted, great debates are occurring over whether time and money are necessary for restructuring. Many point to business as a model to show that additional investments are needed and that results will not appear overnight. Others believe that waste in the system needs to be recaptured. Few are willing to develop the right balance between reality and expectations.

Schools Must Please Everyone, and Few Believe It's That Bad

When looking at a complete reorganization of schooling, some hasten to point out that many eyes are watching. Unlike private corporations where fairly autonomous chief executives and boards of directors can make decisions in relative privacy, educators operate under constraints imposed by state and local boards and cannot limit media or citizen access to information. "Restructuring education . . . will be much more difficult than restructuring corporations. Education is a public institution with public visibility. An immense number of groups and organizations are powerful stakeholders" (The Business Roundtable, 1990, p. v).

Indeed, restructuring and school-site decision making could be at odds with each other. Councils composed of parents, teachers, and community members are frequently formed as part of decentralization. This, in turn, leads to large numbers of people among whom consensus must be reached. Although the buy-in of a large constituency is necessary to implement change, it also makes it more difficult to make tough choices. Many parents are reluctant to change the educational system while their children are still in school.

Although many propose that parent involvement and community involvement are key reform ingredients, others contend that parents may also represent a stumbling block to restructuring. When a well-regarded suburban high school near St. Louis decided to restructure, parents balked while noting they did not want their children involved in an experiment (Olson, 1990a). In Arizona, several similar experiences illustrate this point. One situation involved parental resistance toward a new state performance-based student assessment program. The feeling portrayed at legislative hearings by these middle-class parents was that because the current testing program works well for their children, it should be left alone, or at a minimum, implementation should be delayed. Another case involved a group of upper-middle-class parents who were adamant that new instructional methods, such as cooperative learning, were being implemented for the benefit of only at-risk children, not their children. In this particular case, the resistance of the parents was so strong that the principal was reassigned to the central office. Finally, a concerned mother recently questioned her district's possible decision to eliminate courses that "track" students (e.g., remedial math, regular math, advanced math). This parent is well educated and knows the dangers of the current system, but was worried about losing the advanced classes for her own children.

Embedded in these parents' concerns is the notion that the educational system is really not that bad. Louis Gerstner (1991), chairman and chief executive officer of RJR Nabisco, indicates that one reason restructuring is so difficult is that America clings to the notion that our educational system is the best in the world. Too many believe that the crisis has not touched their community. Risk-taking is neither encouraged by parents nor rewarded by the system. Gerstner advocates making every citizen aware of the strong connection between education, our economic competitiveness, our quality of life, and the future of our democracy.

Gallup Poll data support this notion. In 1991, while only 21% of the respondents gave public schools nationally a grade of "A" or "B," 42% gave schools in their own community similar marks. When asked about the school their oldest children attend, 72% gave it high marks (Elam, Rose, & Gallup, 1991). International comparisons also support this concept. Using the research of Harold Stevenson from the University of Michigan, Finn (1991) indicates that American students, when compared to students in Japan and Taiwan, give themselves top ratings when predicting their mathematics performance in spite of the reality that American students consistently score lower. American parents are also more satisfied with their children's schooling, demonstrated by 91% giving positive ratings to their schools, compared to only 42% of the Chinese mothers and 39% of the Japanese mothers sampled.

Therefore, the debate on restructuring schooling is driven by both the perception of American parents that education is satisfactory in their own backyard and by the need to please a very large constituency. As noted by the National Governors' Association (1991):

> State leaders are faced with a double-edged sword—trying to convince the public that there is a crisis in education while supporting educators, parents, and students. . . . It is indeed a challenge to convince the public that schools are failing students at the top of the scale as well as those at the bottom. (p. 11)

Basic Value Conflicts

Many underlying principles come into play as part of the restructuring/decentralization debate. It order to provide maximum local autonomy for designing a system best suited for a specific community's constituents, it is believed that one must sacrifice some aspects of equity, excellence, accountability, and efficiency.

Centralization is intended to enhance *equity* by reducing resource disparities and allowing flexibility to transfer resources where they are needed most. In addition, Weiler (1990) notes that modern labor markets and communication systems are now requiring even more uniform competencies, skills, and certifications at the national and international level; the implication is that some centralization is necessary for student *excellence.* On the other hand, decentralization is said to allow diversity and the recognition of different cultural environments. Overall, there is a basic tension between decentralization on one hand and the tendency of the modern state to assert or reassert centralized control over the educational system on the other.

Holding schools *accountable* under a decentralized system also becomes more difficult, especially because most of the current accountability measures focus on inputs rather than outputs. Standardized curricula, tests, and programs have been easy to monitor. Creative systems, whereby one school becomes nongraded, another is year-round, and a third provides instruction and day-care from 6 a.m. to 9 p.m.—all within the same school district—are more difficult to compare and monitor. In addition, pluralist societies face a lack of consensus on the objectives of education and specific evaluation criteria. Current debates over possible national assessments, as presented in Chapter 4, will clearly illustrate this point. Although a great deal of work is being completed on new authentic assessments that focus on student outcomes instead of inputs, most states are years away from accomplishing this task. In addition, consensus on relevant evaluation criteria may never occur in our country.

Finally, in reference to *efficiency,* greater local autonomy is expected to result in better utilization of resources, and better products should result. However, decentralization may involve lost efficiencies due to diminished economies of scale. Decisions can be made much more quickly by one person or a small group of people. Indeed, corporations that take on major reorganization see profits reduced during the first few years due both to the initial investment in training and to the loss of efficiency. Many school critics believe that restructuring will immediately save money and that those savings can be applied toward other educational needs, such as the support of at-risk students. Others debate whether a school system will ever reap the financial gains of a better product; well-educated students benefit society as a whole, but do not necessarily bring additional revenues to the school.

Overall, most believe that schools need to become more effective in educating students and that restructuring/decentralizing will help accomplish this goal. Conservatives note that within very large school districts, a decrease in central office administration will provide a great deal of additional resources for schools. Liberals contend that a central office staff may be necessary to safeguard equity for students and that not all functions provided are a waste. Transportation, maintenance, personnel functions (e.g., fingerprint and certification checks), bidding and purchasing, collective bargaining, paperwork and evaluations for state and federal programs, and the like still need to be completed. A clash of such values is partially responsible for so few truly restructured educational systems.

Real and Perceived Roadblocks

Although restructuring and decentralization activities would give teachers additional authority, critics hasten to note that many teacher organizations are at most "lukewarm to decentralization" (Anrig, 1985, p. 126). These organizations are concerned that if all power is moved from the central office to the school level, then collective bargaining would also move to the school level. There is an advantage to bargaining in large groups, and many fear the loss of hard-earned job security rights. However, most district-level collective bargaining agreements restrict site-based management activities. For example, many contain constraints on hours of employment, require compensation for additional responsibilities such as committee work, and prescribe uniform practices across schools within a given district. Critics note that teacher associations are protecting their turf and not focusing on the needs of students. In response, the associations emphasize that radical change brings chaos, fear, and frustration as teachers are told that the system for which they were trained and in which they have worked for many years is obsolete. Time is needed for these changes to become fruitful.

Many have indicated that schools and districts are being prevented from restructuring and/or decentralizing due to restrictive state laws. Others illustrate that at least 14 states have implemented provisions whereby districts or schools can seek waivers from most state laws and regulations; however, very few substantive requests have been made. Either the state barrier was more of a perception than a reality, or a lack of creativity prevented people from moving beyond what they currently have. Chris Pipho from the Education Commission of the States says: "It's like opening the gate to the pasture and the cows—the school people—are so used to staying in there, they just look at the open gate and wonder what it means" (Dunlap, 1991, p. 25). Beyond the creativity issue, collective bargaining agreements developed as part of local control appear to be more of a real barrier to restructuring efforts than most state laws and regulations.

Top-Down Versus Bottom-Up Reforms

There is great debate regarding the best way to accomplish major restructuring changes, and unfortunately, limited research exists to map the way. Should the mandate come down from above, or should the top simply allow, encourage, and guide those at the bottom to change? Or is some combination of these the best? The current mode of thinking is that those at the top (e.g., state or district level) should set high standards and develop accountability systems to measure outcomes, but allow those at the bottom (districts or schools) to determine the best way to accomplish these standards, given the dynamics of each community.

For example, let us briefly review two completely different approaches to the creation of school-based decision making by comparing recent reforms in Chicago and Florida. In 1988 the Illinois legislature enacted provisions requiring the creation of school councils at each of 594 schools in the Chicago public schools. Chicago's system had been declared the worst in the nation by former Secretary of Education William Bennett, and it was believed that radical steps were necessary (Wohlstetter & McCurdy, 1991). The legislation specified the exact composition of each council to be six parents, two teachers, two community members, and the principal as ex officio member. This council was given the authority to hire/fire the principal, approve the school budget, and oversee curriculum and instructional decisions for its school. One key goal was to weaken the power of the central office and the strong principal's association by placing a great deal of power in the hands of parents. The school council has full authority to retain or dismiss the principal; during the first 2 years, nearly 20% of the principals were released. It has been viewed as the "Chicago Revolution," and lawsuits and ongoing controversy continue. A major concern is whether mandated decentralization can be effective.

The Dade County public school system in Florida offers a different approach. With more than 250,000 students and an annual budget exceeding $1 billion, this school system is the fourth-largest in the nation. Developed jointly by the teachers' association and the district administration in 1988, the "School Based Management/Shared Decision Making" model has been phased in over time and is well received by most involved. School site councils of varying compositions now have control over curriculum, day-to-day school operations, and ever-growing portions of the school's budget. More than 80% of their budgets are on the table for discussion since school councils have increased discretion in hiring (Dunlap, 1991). Final authority over personnel still rests with the local board. Many contend that this approach is far better than a state imposed top-down model; however, the process is time-consuming, and similar changes are occurring in too few districts across the country.

Moving Ahead

Changing America's education factories from an industrial paradigm to a high-tech model has only begun, even with extraordinary economic pressures to do so. We have a Model-T system trying to work in a space-age world. Too many believe that the old assembly line design of schooling served them well and therefore does not require radical overhaul. In addition, there are basic value conflicts. Everyone wants excellence, but many balk at providing additional resources until the system is more efficient. Conversely, others note that the system cannot become more efficient until additional resources are provided for retooling. Liberty plays a role since some believe restructuring will provide more real choices for parents. Many are concerned that these types of experiments will do little to foster equity for students. Issues such as time, money, apathy, basic societal values, real and perceived barriers, and limited research continue to drive the debate.

Overall, our educational system must be radically changed; the world has changed while schooling has not. Until a vast social movement develops, limited systemic restructuring will occur. Former New Mexico Governor Garrey Carruthers (1990) remarks:

Restructuring is about sharing responsibility for success, not finding reasons for failure. It's about rebuilding the system, not tearing one another apart. It's about every one of us breaking out of our own box and finding new ways of thinking about and, more importantly, doing something about, education. (pp. 22-23)

4

How Can We Hold the System Accountable?

Introduction

As one of the educational buzzwords of the 1980s, "accountability," continues to be an integral aspect of educational policy debates. Hardly a month goes by without newspaper reports of yet another international test of students' academic achievement where the United States has ranked near the bottom. Recent data from the 1990 National Assessment of Educational Progress (NAEP) math exams illustrate that half of today's graduating high school seniors appear to have mathematics skills that do not extend beyond simple problem solving with whole numbers. Few are graduating with the skills necessary for the fastest-growing occupations or for college work (National Center for Education Statistics, 1991b). The "Johnny can't read" saga continues as more than $250 million per year is spent by corporations to remediate the basic skills of many workers (Tifft, 1991). Although valid reasons can be offered for some concerns, the problem is real and significant.

As with many other educational reform issues, the question is no longer "Should we be holding schools more accountable?" but "How can we achieve accountability?" In addition, many wonder who is responsible. Most citizens would immediately blame teachers, administrators, and school board members; others point to the problems in society and the lack of parental support and involvement. Some indict students and their lack of effort. A few note that the structure is flawed and that little more can be expected than what is currently being accomplished.

This is not to say that no data are being collected from our schools. Instead,

> The assessment of education in the country suffered from much the same disease as the system itself: mixed, spotty, confusing information, gathered by a welter of public and private agencies, using tests of all stripes—standardized and nonstandard, normed and unnormed, formative and summative, essay and multiple choice, local and national, given by virtually every teacher, some districts, many states, and even national agencies. [However,] for all the effort, the nation still knows precious little about the productivity of its schools. (Doyle, Cooper, & Trachtman, 1991, p. 87-88)

As one example, the National Commission on Testing and Public Policy reports that each year 127 million standardized tests are administered to K-12 students, with 20 million school days devoted to such testing (Educational Testing Service, 1990). This equates to approximately three tests per year per student. Indeed, during the past decade, nearly every state has initiated some form of testing.

The concern, however, is that comprehensive accountability systems have not yet been developed, although several states are moving forward quickly in this direction. The gathering of information is just part of the process. Lacking is a systemic linkage of testing to curriculum, curriculum to goals, and outcomes to rewards or sanctions. Several key components of an "accountability loop" currently driving the debate include:

- Goals—What do we want the schools to accomplish?
- Predetermined standards—How will we know if the goals are met?
- Assessments—How will progress be measured fairly and accurately?
- Rewards/sanctions—What happens to those schools that consistently fail to make progress or those that exceed the established standards?

Also driving the debate are decisions regarding the type of accountability techniques to implement. Romzek and Dubnick (1987) have identified four strategies for achieving public accountability: bureaucratic, legal, professional, and political. Bureaucratic and professional strategies are internal organizational control mechanisms and reflect a belief that the educational process can be routinized; political and legal strategies are external and depend on motivation and goal-oriented behavior. As the public policy debate moves toward a top-down, bottom-up approach, a blend of external political and legal strategies (e.g., setting high standards and requiring public report cards) and internal professional strategies (e.g., decentralizing to allow teachers to improve outcomes) is materializing. Highlights of the debate follow.

National and State Goal Setting

Without clear outcome goals and standards, it is nearly impossible to hold schools accountable. An overall goal of recent reforms has been to improve the education of students; however, this means different things to different people. Indeed, many states developed goals during the 1980s, but these were seldom used to guide policy decisions. However, steps at both the state and national levels to more carefully define educational goals are under way. At the 1989 Governors' Education Summit with President Bush, six national educational goals were adopted. Specifically, by the year 2000:

1. All children in America will start school ready to learn.
2. The high school graduation rate will increase to at least 90%.
3. American students will leave Grades 4, 8, and 12 having demonstrated competency in challenging subject matter including English, mathematics, science, history, and geography; and every school in America will ensure that all students learn to use their minds well, so they may be prepared for responsible citizenship, further learning, and productive employment in our modern economy.
4. U.S. students will be first in the world in science and mathematics achievement.
5. Every adult American will be literate and will possess the knowledge and skills necessary to compete in a global economy and exercise the rights and responsibilities of citizenship.
6. Every school in America will be free of drugs and violence and will offer a disciplined environment conducive to learning.

Although volumes have been written criticizing these goals (e.g., they cannot be accomplished by the year 2000; certain subjects such as fine arts and vocational education were not included), they are important because, for the first time, the nation has a set of written educational goals against which progress can be measured. Gallup Poll data from 1990 and 1991 illustrate that the public strongly supports all the goals, but expresses profound skepticism about attaining them by the year 2000. For example, while 90% of the respondents rated the first goal as either a very high or a high priority for our country, 47% noted that it was unlikely or very unlikely that the goal will be achieved (Elam et al., 1991).

As of February 1992, 32 states had formally adopted the national goals as guides for their own state goals. Annual state comparison "report cards" of progress are under way, providing an added incentive for states to formulate their plans and activities around these six goals. Many view these goals as minimums and have developed additional goal areas and/or have adopted more specific language; others believe they are unattainable and are purely campaign rhetoric. Nonetheless, many believe that the next step for the nation and for each state is to determine exactly how progress toward these goals will be measured and then develop assessment instruments to accomplish this task. This is much easier said than done.

National Standards and Assessments

As noted in the introduction, vast testing and data collection already occurs in American schools, but it is "largely a patchwork, with some students taking one examination and others another. The United States lacks a national system of achievement testing that would allow comparisons of a student's or school's performance with students and schools across the nation" (Cheney, 1991, p. 2). This patchwork of assessment exists because the U.S. system is indeed decentralized, with states, not the federal government, having control over education. To this end, 50 different state and thousands of local district assessment/accountability systems operate in this nation. Since the advent of the national goals, many are discussing the need for a national test or testing system. Although most agree our current system is in disarray, there is concern that the balance of national and state power could lean too heavily toward the national level.

Leading the discussion is the National Education Goals Panel (NEGP). Chaired by Governor Roy Romer of Colorado, this panel's job is to oversee the development and implementation of a national education progress reporting system. The third national education goal—the assessment of student achievement—has captured much of the panel's attention. The debate focuses on the possibility of setting national goals and initiating a national test.

In response to the great controversy on this topic, Congress created the National Council on Education Standards and Testing to determine the desirability and feasibility of national standards and testing. Lewis (1991) reports that the council was advised by members of Congress to consider nine issues that serve to highlight the debate:

1. The benefits and liabilities of imposing uniform national standards, a national test, or a system of national exams.
2. Any evidence that national standards and tests promote improvements in educational achievement.
3. Whether national standards are appropriate, given the wide variations in available resources across states.
4. Whether additional support for special needs students (e.g., handicapped, LEP) should be part of any effort to implement national standards and testing.
5. Whether national tests intended for instructional improvement could be used for such unintended purposes as tracking.
6. Whether consensus is possible or likely on particular sets of standards and, if so, whether it can be developed within the specified time.
7. How to develop an open process in which all interested parties have the opportunity to be heard.
8. Whether, given the wide range of student performance in basic academic performance, it is feasible to develop standards that challenge all children to do their best without penalizing those who have had fewer educational opportunities.
9. The feasibility of a national system of tests in terms of validity, reliability, fairness, and cost.

In January 1992 the report of this council, *Raising Standards for American Education,* was unveiled and called for the development of high national student achievement standards and a national assessment system (Rothman, 1992a). However, the report also warned that these standards and assessments should not develop into a national curriculum or a single national test. Instead, the standards should serve as the core of understanding that all students need to acquire, but not everything that a student must learn. In addition, equity must be of primary concern to educators and policymakers; providing genuine opportunity for all students to achieve high standards is a national moral imperative. Overall, the report generally moved in the direction espoused by many previous critics: general national standards and a national assessment "system," not a single national "test." These standards and assessments would be voluntary, not mandatory, for states.

Because it was a highly political document, however, many compromises were made (Lewis, 1992). Concerns remain about data collection and use. For example, a group of 48 prominent educators and professors have publicized their view that these assessments should be used primarily for teaching and learning, not assigning rewards and sanctions (Rothman, 1992b). Winfield and Woodard (1992) also discuss the problems associated with the potential use of these data to certify job skills for prospective employers. Because resource inequities currently exist among schools, and "non-European racial and ethnic groups" are disproportionately larger in the poorer schools, these tests could be an additional barrier to employment opportunities for those students. Finally, the Office of Technology Assessment, a nonpartisan research congressional agency, warned Congress of the many logistical concerns that have yet to be worked out and of the historical misuse of high-stakes testing (Rothman, 1992c).

Despite these criticisms, Gallup Poll data reveal public support for a stronger national educational agenda. During 1991, 68% supported a standardized national curriculum; 81% favored national achievement standards and goals; 77% wanted their schools to use standardized national tests; and 73% or more supported the development of school, district, state, and national report cards illustrating progress toward the national goals (Elam et al., 1991). This debate will continue, but many believe that national standards and expanding national assessments will be initiated during the next few years. This will represent a major policy shift regarding national and state roles in education. Many believe that, for the sake of excellence, local state control must be reduced. Others fear that greater national influence could hurt the democratic process.

The Debate on Testing

Underlying current debates on national assessment is concern over a history of testing use and misuse in this country. During the past decade, nearly every state has initiated some type of testing program. Many utilize norm-referenced standardized testing, state criterion-referenced tests, or both. Several states have begun the move toward performance-based assessments in a desire to make testing more meaningful for both teachers and policymakers. An analysis of the reasons current assessments are not believed to be adequate will highlight the many difficulties ahead as a new breed of assessments is envisioned.

"Testing" Definitions

First, several definitions are necessary. Generally, *assessment* refers to a larger gathering of data upon which to make valuative decisions, while *tests* or *testing* refers to an instrument or means to gather assessment information. However, because of their similarity, the two terms will be used interchangeably in this chapter.

Standardized, norm-referenced tests are developed to allow the comparison of an individual's scores to those of others who have taken a version of the same test (i.e., the norming group). The tests are designed so that scores are distributed as a bell curve, with a certain percentage of students scoring above the average and a certain percentage below. A student's score does not necessarily reflect what the student knows about a given subject, but how much he or she knows compared to a norming group. These tests usually utilize a multiple-choice format to allow machine scoring. Common tests used by states are the Iowa Test of Basic Skills (ITBS) and the Standard Achievement Tests (SAT). These tests are developed and sold commercially to states and districts across the nation. Therefore, the information assessed by any one test may represent just a portion of the curriculum prescribed by any given state or district.

Criterion-referenced tests base item selection on a domain of required knowledge and determine how close the test-taker came to reaching 100% competency (Brown Easton, 1991). A panel of experts usually establishes the percentage of correct responses needed for passing or minimal competence. This means that a student's score represents his or her performance against the total possible number of correct answers, rather than how the student compared to other students. Many states have had criterion-referenced tests developed specifically for their curriculum frameworks. However, one common national test, the National Assessment of Educational Progress (NAEP), was designed to include subject area test items relevant across many state curricula. Criterion-referenced tests still usually contain multiple-choice questions to allow computer scoring.

Finally, *performance-based tests* or *authentic assessments* refer to tests that have moved "beyond the bubble sheet." These tests no longer rely on multiple-choice questions for which one correct answer needs to be placed on computer sheets, but instead require students to write essays, solve math problems, conduct science experiments, or show a portfolio of art work. The consensus is that these assessments more closely match real world tasks. In addition, performance-based testing solves concern over "teaching to the test" since it is the kind of test that you want teachers to prepare students for. However, the scoring of these tests is far more expensive because humans, not machines, are used and it involves subjectivity despite clearly defined scoring criteria (i.e., rubrics). The Advanced Placement (AP) examination taken by high school students for college credit is one example of this type of testing.

A Brief History of Educational Testing in the United States

Berlak (1992) indicates that the roots of mass testing can be traced to testing of more than 2 million conscripts during World War I, using an adaption of the Stanford-Binet, the nation's first IQ test. The idea was that this test could provide the military with the scientific basis for routing draftees into the jobs that best suited their abilities and could be used to identify and control social deviants. This same thinking and data extracted from the military tests provided a scientific basis for quotas and restrictions set in the National Origins Act of 1924. Berlak notes that the resulting immigrant restrictions favored northern Europeans over southern and eastern Europeans and barred all Japanese, Chinese, and other Asians.

During the 1930s scientific management push within the schools, IQ testing became commonplace. One outcome was that test results were used to place students in special education or remedial classes. Unfortunately, this resulted in a disproportional placement of minorities in these classes. The real explosion of standardized testing, however, occurred during the 1970s, as part of a push for minimal competency standards. During this time Americans perceived a decline in educational standards and demanded a return to the basics. As a result, many states adopted minimum competency testing programs using standardized tests, hoping to ensure that students achieved at least the lowest acceptable minimums.

The 1980s wave of accountability caused many states to either expand their existing testing programs or implement new ones. Testing also became more of a high-stakes issue for students, schools, and districts in that graduation frequently became tied to test scores. School and district test data are now comparatively ranked in the local newspaper, and some administrators' jobs depend on increased scores. As of spring 1991, 47 states had student testing programs, of which 38 used the test results to monitor school districts overall; 23 used the tests as student gatekeeping devices; 20 used them as indicators of the need to remediate; and 9 used them to distribute funds (Educational Testing Service, 1990).

Although most of the testing movement was at the state level, one key assessment activity was occurring nationally. Initiated in 1969, the National Assessment of Educational Progress (NAEP) is a federally funded assessment intended to create a snapshot of educational progress throughout our country. Using random sampling, these assessments were specifically designed so that individual state comparisons could not be made. During the mid-1980s, however, interest in obtaining individual state data came from both the state and national levels. In response, a panel convened by Secretary of Education William Bennett recommended that NAEP begin to make state-by-state comparisons. This led to congressional concerns about state comparisons, federally subsidized competition for the testing industry, and potential test bias against racial and ethnic minorities. What emerged was a two-phase trial expansion in which states could volunteer to participate and be compared. In 1990, 37 states elected to participate in the eight-grade math assessment; 42 states have agreed to join the 1992 math and reading assessment (Jaeger, 1991). However, the use of NAEP data is still banned for comparing individual students, schools, or districts.

The growing use of state testing and the discussion about potential national testing have brought protests from the educational research community. Over the years, studies have shown the negative effects of standardized testing. It was found that basic skills questions served to water down the curriculum because the minimums had become the maximums. As states and districts put more weight on the testing outcomes, teachers began to spend more time preparing for the test and, in many cases, teaching to the test. Many policymakers began to seriously rethink the role of norm-referenced testing as part of an educational accountability system.

In response, several states began to experiment with performance-based assessments tied to high-level curriculum frameworks (e.g., Arizona, California, Vermont). However, this process is difficult due to the costs associated with test development, an ingrained standardized test mentality, and, of course, politics. In Arizona, conservative newspaper editorial writers charged that these new performance-based tests were going to be developed in someone's basement rather than by a trusted testing company. In response, state officials hired the company that sells the Iowa Test of Basic Skills to develop the state's new assessments. Similar political concerns are evident in California, where former Governor George Deukmejian used his line-item veto to kill the California Assessment Program during August 1990 as part of budget cuts and an ongoing political dispute (Pipho, 1991). In January 1991 newly elected Governor Pete Wilson agreed to invest $10 million in a new testing program if it included scores for individual students, an end-of-course test, and common district standards. Although these restrictions appear reasonable, they drive the state program away from a matrix-sampling performance test to an end-of-course test involving every student. Cost and testing time are now elements being worked out. In Kentucky, nearly $30 million is to be appropriated over the next 5 years to fully develop a performance-based assessment program. Programs in Maryland, Connecticut, and Vermont are also under way. Assessment is at the heart of the current educational policy debate since many are viewing the reforms of the 1990s as "outcome driven."

What's Wrong With Standardized Testing?

In a special section in the November 1991 *Phi Delta Kappan,* Darling-Hammond, Shepard, McLaughlin, and other education professors summarize key problems with the standardized tests utilized in America. Their assessments are based upon research conducted during the past two decades of mass testing. Several findings will be highlighted as evidence offered by these scholars regarding problems associated with such testing.

First, when testing becomes high stakes, scores can become inflated, giving a false impression of student achievement. For example, in 1987 a West Virginia physician issued a report indicating that he had surveyed all 50 states and discovered that none was below average at the elementary level on any of the six major nationally normed, commercially available tests. He also indicated that 90% of local school districts claim that their averages exceed the national average, and that more than 70% of the students were told they are performing above the national average (Finn, 1991). Nicknamed the "Lake Wobegon Effect" after Garrison Keillor's radio show, where all the children in a fictional town are above average, this report attracted national attention. Since norm-referenced tests are designed so that approximately half the students should be above average while the other half are below average, this finding was truly amazing. Indeed, upon investigation by the U.S. Department of Education, it was determined that current norm-referenced tests overstate achievement in many schools, districts, and states. Several reasons were identified, including old norms and the effort of districts to prepare their students. Test-makers acknowledged the lack of industry standards at the time, and some believed overinflation of scores was linked to the desire to sell large numbers of tests (Brown Easton, 1991).

Second, high-stakes standardized tests narrow the curriculum toward basic skills and reinforce outdated learning theories. Testing in the United States is primarily controlled by commercial publishers who produce norm-referenced, multiple-choice tests designed to measure students' basic skills cheaply and efficiently; existing tests were never intended to support or enhance instruction. Although the 1980s push for excellence attempted to emphasize the need for developing students' higher-order cognitive abilities, the national standardized tests remained focused on basic skills. Because many teachers and administrators felt pressure to improve test scores, more time was dedicated to teaching basic skills. This is confirmed by Darling-Hammond (1991), who notes that between 1972 and 1980, public schools showed a decline in the use of such teaching methods as student-centered discussions, essay writing, and research projects or laboratory work. As a result, scores on basic skills tests have improved, while scores on assessments of higher-order thinking skills have steadily declined.

In reference to learning theory, Shepard (1991) notes that norm-referenced standardized tests are based on a premise that complex, higher-order skills must be broken down into constituent, prerequisite skills that must be learned prior to understanding complex thought and insight. In contrast, evidence from cognitive psychology shows that all learning requires thinking and active construction by the learner. Teachers are currently providing daily skills instruction in formats that closely resemble standardized tests' focus on isolated facts and skills. Simply stated, research has shown that *tested* content tends to be taught to the exclusion of *nontested* material, and the current tested content does not support higher-order thinking skills or other complex tasks.

A third problem is that students harmed most by these basic skills tests are those they were intended to help most. This raises serious equity concerns. Schools use the outcomes of these tests to identify students needing additional assistance and to place them in remedial programs. A system of "tracking" has evolved, with continued emphasis on drill and practice. These students are seldom exposed to nontested modes of thinking and performance, such as reading books, discussing ideas, writing, and engaging in creative learning tasks, because these activities are reserved until the teacher is sure that students can master the basics found on the test. Some states and districts have enacted policies requiring that test scores be used as the criteria for promotion to the next grade level. However, studies have shown that repeating a grade does not help students achieve and, in fact, has been shown to substantially increase the likelihood of a student's becoming a dropout (Shepard, 1991). In addition, some states currently require students to demonstrate mastery of minimum skills prior to graduation. While this is a noteworthy goal, the mode of assessment is very important in that cultural and gender bias still exist.

Finally, standardized basic skills tests have reduced the professional knowledge and status of teachers. Studies have shown that many teachers are troubled by the discord between the instructional methods they are forced to adopt (e.g., worksheets) and their own training and beliefs about children's learning (Shepard, 1991). Tests drive mandated curricula, textbooks, and standards, which in turn serve to teacher-proof tasks. Teachers are degraded and deskilled by high-stakes standardized testing.

These are just a few of the reasons many education researchers and practitioners are concerned about the implementation of a national test that might promote further testing abuses. An overriding fear is that the lowest common denominator of skills will be developed in order to become acceptable to all 50 states. Many believe that the move to performance-based testing will solve past problems, but are extremely doubtful that the kind of funding necessary to develop, implement, and grade these tests will be forthcoming. For example, it cost approximately $150 per pupil tested to administer and score the pilot 1990

NAEP fourth-grade mathematics exam. Multiplied by more than 40 million American students, this equals $6 billion for just one math assessment. Economies of scale will bring this cost down, but moving away from machine scoring is extremely expensive.

Cost, however, is not the only roadblock. There is an underlying lack of trust as teachers and professors point out their concerns over testing. Many contend that these people are simply trying to protect their turf. For years, educators have criticized almost every test that has been proposed, while at the same time failing to develop assessments that will work. Policymakers have required the use of norm-referenced testing primarily because little else was available at the time for state-wide application. Some contend that if educational researchers had spent less time trying to prevent testing and more time in developing better assessments, the current battle would not be occurring.

What About Testing in Other Countries?

Since the test scores of U.S. students are frequently compared to those of students across the world, it is relevant to review other countries' testing systems to see what lessons can be learned. This section highlights information on models used in France, Germany, England, and Japan, as extracted from *National Tests: What Other Countries Expect Their Students to Know*, prepared by Lynn Cheney (1991) of the National Endowment for the Humanities.

Tests used in these four countries are very different than those employed in the United States. Whereas the United States is focused primarily on norm-referenced testing, tests in France, Germany, and England are criterion-referenced, comparing students to a set of criteria or standards. Only the Japanese system makes extensive use of multiple-choice exams; the other three countries use performance-based assessments, in which students must write their responses, provide oral defense, or, as in the German system, give practical demonstrations in subjects such as music and the natural sciences. Unlike the U.S. tests, exam content comprises not only events relevant to their own country, but also culture and historical events across the world.

Another difference is the strong role played by their national governments in that each has a common examination system for its country. France and Japan have rigorously defined national curricula and tests, while England has had national examinations for many decades and is now developing a national curriculum for the first time. In Germany, although each separate state develops its own curriculum and is allowed to select specific exam questions for the national exam, a coordinating body works to make curricula and examinations comparable across the country.

Within these four countries, national tests are administered when students are older and the outcomes have real significance. In France, most students enter upper secondary schools called *lycées* at age 15 or 16. Within these 3-year programs, a student concentrates on a specialized course of study (e.g., economics, liberal arts, chemistry) and prepares for the *baccalauréat* examination on that area. Only upon passage of this examination is a student permitted to enroll in a university. According to 1990 figures, 67% of all students enrolled in a *lycée,* of whom 50% took the *baccalauréat* exam and 38.5% passed. The French government has set a goal for the year 2000 to have 90% of students reach the *baccalauréat* level.

In Germany, students intending to go to a university usually attend *Gymnasien,* schools that go through grade 13 and conclude with an examination known as the *Abitur.* Together with the grades earned in the 12th and 13th years of school, the *Abitur* determines university eligibility for students. The general form of the *Abitur* is consistent throughout the country, but the specific content is determined by education ministries in the various states. Students choose four subjects in which to be examined from three categories of knowledge: languages, literature, and the arts; social sciences; and mathematics, natural sciences, and technology. In 1986, only 23.7% of the relevant age group qualified for university entrance.

In England and Wales, 16-year-olds finish compulsory schooling and take examinations that lead to the General Certificate of Secondary Education (GCSE). Tied to the new national curriculum being developed, the GCSE is also evolving. Currently, all students are required to take GCSEs in three subjects (English, math, and science); in addition, they can choose to have other subjects areas assessed (history, geography, technology, and foreign languages). At this point, students may choose to continue in a specialized 2-year course of secondary education leading to the advanced or "A-level" exams typically taken for university admission. In 1989 only 22% passed one or more A-level exams; 12% passed three or more. Both the GCSE and A-level exams are developed and administered by regional and university examining boards; thus, not all exams are identical, but a national coordinating board keeps them to a common standard. Current curriculum and assessment revisions include broadening the curriculum for the last 2 years of secondary school and combining teacher-assessed course work with examination scores.

Finally, in Japan, all students wishing to attend a national or public university take the "Test of the National Center for University Entrance Examination." This test covers five areas of knowledge: Japanese, humanities/social sciences, mathematics, science, and foreign language. Within each area, students have some options, depending upon their high school course of study and the requirements of the university they wish to attend. At most universities, factors such as grades and/or additional university tests are taken into account in addition to the test. Competition is intense in that the 1990 ratio of test-takers to available university slots was almost four to one. Most students attend commercially run cram schools called "juku" after school and on weekends. Some who perform poorly on the tests will spend a year or more studying to take the exam again. Unlike exams in England, France, and Germany, this test is multiple-choice and stresses rote learning.

As one can see, these educational systems vastly differ from those in the United States in terms of the importance of testing and the types of tests offered. Although outcomes of the U.S. educational system are frequently compared to those of other countries, there are vast structural differences among these systems. Most British and German students are finished with their formal high school education at the end of 10th grade and are tracked into the academic or vocational world; as a result, only a portion of their students remain to take Grade 12 academic exams. In Japan, vast cultural differences exist in that academic learning takes precedence over everything else and most 12th-grade students will have received nearly 2 years of additional education, compared to those in the United States, simply because their school year contains 243 days, instead of America's 180 days. Because of these and other differences, many urge caution when making test score comparisons. This information should not be viewed as excuses for the low U.S. test scores, but should be used to create an awareness of disparate populations as international comparisons are made. Indeed, many other countries are also attempting to improve their current systems. For example, Japanese authorities have proposed reducing their school year by 11 days in an attempt to reduce the Saturday school requirement.

Another key difference is that the United States has the most egalitarian system in the world for K-12 and higher education, in which Americans take great pride (Finn 1991; Kirst, 1984). The down side is that, except for a small percentage of very selective universities, students need little more than a high school diploma and the tuition money to enter the higher education system. Some universities require students to take an aptitude test such as the SAT or ACT, to have certain grades, or to have a specific class ranking. However, these aptitude tests focus more on innate ability and general cognitive functioning than on specific knowledge and skills learned in school, and grades or class rankings may bear little relationship to what is actually learned in school.

In reference to the workplace, testing and grades play a major role in many countries, but not so in the United States. Large Japanese firms, for example, hire many entry-level workers directly out of high schools and base their selections on grades and exam scores. In America, those going directly into the workplace are asked only to indicate on the application that they graduated from high school. Grades or transcripts are seldom, if ever, mentioned.

This section is not intended to criticize the entrance requirements of universities or workplaces in the United States, but it is offered to illustrate the importance of high-stakes testing and grades in other countries. While the United States does indeed have cause to be proud of providing access to higher education for nearly all students, little incentive exists for students to do well on exams. Indeed, stories abound of high school seniors skipping school on the day state testing is completed, or of students forming geometric shapes on their bubble sheets instead of attempting to answer the questions. Although many are concerned about high-stakes testing, others believe the stakes are not high enough (Cheney, 1991). Many see this as an elitist view since it could diminish equal educational opportunity for many students. In addition, high-stakes testing can take a toll on students, as evidenced by the suicide rates among youngsters in Japan and by early career tracking in Germany. On the other hand, some say the only real way to have equity in the United States is to establish extremely high standards for all students; to provide additional support for those in need; and to hold students, teachers, parents, and others responsible for outcomes.

The Future of Testing in the United States

McLaughlin (1991) states: "Test-based accountability or high-stakes testing is an idea that has come to seem inevitable. . . . [It's like] an 18-wheeler careening down a steep mountain grade" (p. 248). McLaughlin's remarks show that even high-stakes testing critics realize that some form of a national testing system is probable, but hope that a firm commitment will be made to follow the performance-based assessment route. This will require time and funding, but if solid outcome measures are that important, then perhaps it is necessary for our country to make this investment. Some are calling for a "1%" solution, whereby 1% of all educational funding would be earmarked for assessment. Although this does not seem like much, it would represent at least 20 times what is currently being spent in most states. McLaughlin summarizes a common viewpoint of her colleagues:

> [G]o slow . . . the version of testing now on the policy table—high-stakes testing—matters a great deal to the quality and character of America's classrooms. Unlike most reform initiatives, which fiddle at the margins of the classroom or which depend upon acceptance by the classroom teacher, reform that relies on accountability and high-stakes tests reaches into the heart of the undertaking. . . . the interaction of teachers, students, and subject matter. Tests could benefit and support these interactions, but the technology is not ready yet. (p. 251)

Nonetheless, the process is moving ahead. The National Education Goals Panel initially promised that the first national assessments would be on-line by 1994. Panel chairman Governor Romer noted that if America can go to the Persian Gulf and, in 6 weeks, conduct Desert Storm, then our country can develop a good test in fewer than 6 years (Rothman, 1992a). Leadership of the American Federation of Teachers agrees it is important to move ahead since the status quo is unacceptable. Many note that excessive emphasis is being placed on what could go wrong, rather than what could go right if mass performance-based testing were developed and implemented. Counter-responses state that more development and research are necessary before we do something risky and untried with more than 40 million students.

Although this section has summarized the policy debate over using student testing, many issues raised are also applicable to discussions over teacher testing. Rather than repeating these points, it is simply important to realize that the frenzy to implement teacher testing during the 1980s equaled that of student testing. As of 1988, 29 states required undergraduate students to pass a test prior to admission into teacher education programs; 37 states required the passage of a test for both new and experienced teachers as they seek certification or recertification; and some required test passage for career advancement (Doyle et al., 1991). In Texas, teachers attempting to move up their career ladder must pass a master-teacher examination; during the first testing period, less than 2% (42 of 2,603) teachers passed (Bradley, 1991). Numerous lawsuits have been filed because teachers lost their jobs over failure to pass tests that many believe are biased and have little to do with the act of teaching. As states move away from top-down mandates, the emphasis on teacher testing is subsiding, and some states are modifying or eliminating the requirement (e.g., Arizona); however, many states are still embroiled in the debate.

Overall, many arguments against student and teacher testing are based on pragmatic considerations and research results showing harmful effects. Even if these concerns are understood by testing supporters, they are usually willing to forge ahead because they believe the need to hold students and educators more accountable is essential to reforming the system. Overall, far too little emphasis has been placed on developing testing systems that are affordable (e.g., student sampling only at upper grade levels), which measure the essential critical thinking skills (e.g., performance-based), and which have real meaning for teachers and students. Compared to the comprehensive systems in many other countries, the United States is far behind.

Teacher and School Rewards and Sanctions

Taking the accountability/testing debate one step further, most agree that there should be consequences, both good and bad, for those who succeed or fail at producing appropriate educational outcomes. If schools and districts are expected to operate more like a business and compete with private schools, then perhaps they should be able to make a profit as well to go bankrupt. These are foreign phrases to public organizations, especially education, since everyone knows that educators did not choose their profession for the salary potential. Instead, conventional wisdom states that altruism and love of children or a subject area attracted most teachers to the field. However, as education has lost its market of the most talented women, and as educators are having to develop market-niche schools of choice, many realize that a different set of circumstances may need to govern rewards and sanctions within the educational system. Unfortunately, the lack of quality assessments has caused current reward and sanction systems to focus more on inputs and processes (e.g., how well a teacher teaches or how well a district uses its money) than on outcomes (e.g., student learning). This section examines the debate as it reviews several existing (or planned) individual and group reward and sanctions systems.

Merit Pay and Career Ladder Systems

Within the educational setting, individual rewards in the form of merit pay or career ladders for teachers have already gone through at least their second historical cycle. Prior to the 1930s, salary inequities existed in that men were paid more than women, and high school teachers more than elementary school teachers. Hard-fought battles for equity led to the existing "lock step" salary schedule used by most districts. This type of compensation system bases salaries strictly on years of experience and the number of educational credits obtained. Performance and teaching assignments play no role in determining salaries. For example, two teachers, both with master's degrees and 8 years' experience in the district, will receive identical salaries for their teaching responsibilities (except for extra duty assignments, like coaching). At first glance, this appears to be fair, except that one of these teachers could be the district's teacher of the year, while the other teacher does just enough to get by. During the 1960s and 1970s, some individual schools experimented with merit pay and career ladder plans, but most systems failed due to quota systems, the lack of sound evaluation instruments, and union objections to anything that had the potential to treat teachers unequally.

Merit pay programs generally involve teachers' receiving a bonus to their regular salary for outstanding performance of existing teaching responsibilities. Career ladder programs establish a process whereby career progression can occur for teachers (e.g., promotion to higher levels within the teaching ranks). Teachers may be asked to take on additional and/or more difficult teaching responsibilities, such as mentoring beginning teachers or working with at-risk students. There are salary stipends, but they are usually differentiated based on levels of performance. Most early merit pay and career ladder programs focused on evaluating the act of teaching (e.g., classroom performance), while many now have moved toward evaluations based on student outcomes.

During the 1980s many states became involved either by mandating that every district implement a merit pay or career ladder system (e.g., Florida, Tennessee, Texas) or by offering financial incentives to districts that wished to move in this direction (e.g., Arizona, Utah). Some programs encountered a great deal of difficulty, especially those using state evaluators, or those focused primarily on additional paperwork and "dog and pony" classroom observations. Strong opposition was mounted from teacher unions for several reasons—fears that teachers were competing with each other, biased evaluations, and excessive paperwork (i.e., jumping through hoops). Strong opposition and fiscal constraints caused several states to enact, but never fund, their performance-based compensation programs (e.g., Alabama, Georgia, Kentucky).

On the other hand, several states experienced success, as shown by increased test scores and teacher satisfaction. In Arizona, locally developed pilot programs resulted in student achievement gains beyond those achieved in non-career ladder districts. In Utah, the majority of participating teachers indicated that the program had made teaching more attractive, had a positive impact on their own delivery of instruction, and had at least a moderately positive influence on student achievement (Cornett & Gaines, 1992). Even with state fiscal constraints, of the six states that actually funded programs in 1986, five have made substantial financial and program expansions due to perceived program success.

Overall, however, the country's track record with individual teacher reward systems has been modest at best. Less than 15% of the states support such programs, and the overall assessment therein is still sketchy. Strong criticisms of these programs exist due to program logistics (e.g., paperwork) and in part because people with negative comments tend to be more vocal (e.g., writing letters to the legislature and newspaper) than those with positive comments. Since only a few states undertook objective, third-party evaluations of these programs, data on the outcomes of these programs are limited. Underlying questions are whether one individual can be held responsible for a student's learning, and if so, how this can be measured accurately and objectively without pitting one teacher against another.

Although many states have chosen to fund other types of less threatening programs such as mentor teacher activities, "the notion of tying rewards to individual teachers to results of students is an area where few states have dared to tread" (Cornett & Gaines, 1992, p. 12). Arizona was noted by these authors as one of the few exceptions. In this state, the expansion and permanence of career ladder legislation have been due to both evaluation data showing student achievement increases and a network of teachers effectively communicating how the program had changed their professional lives. What had begun as a program to reward good teachers had evolved into a program that empowered teachers and caused them to focus on student outcomes.

School-Based Rewards

The concept of "group" rewards continues to gain acceptance as an alternative to merit pay or career ladder programs. Operating on the premise that this type of program will encourage greater collegiality, at least 10 states have moved in this direction; however, only a few states allow school rewards to be used for teacher bonuses (Cornett & Gains, 1992). In most cases, the additional bonus funding can be used only on items such as instructional materials or conference travel as determined by the school-site personnel. Several other states have such laws on the books, but have never funded the programs (e.g., Colorado's Excellent Schools Program), or have had to reduce program funding (e.g., Indiana, New York). Few comprehensive evaluations of these programs have been undertaken, but the general feeling is that many of these programs are not creating fundamental systemic changes, due in part to the small amounts of money per school and continued distrust of the selection criteria.

Albert Shanker (1990), president of the AFT, has proposed an "Incentive Schools Program" that would include significant monetary rewards and competition among schools. He proposed that a 5-year national program be initiated where, at its conclusion, the top 10% of the most improved schools would receive at least $15,000 per staff member. (Note: This money would have been generated from investing the $500 million that President Bush had requested in 1990 be used for merit schools.) Participating schools would require a great deal of freedom from both state and district regulations. Shanker envisions that decentralization would occur, individual choice schools would be established, and overall system improvements would be the result. He admits that many logistical issues remain—such as the development of a sound assessment process—but that a program such as this is necessary to promote self-renewal in our schools.

As highlighted above, little real, large-scale individual or group reward activity has been accomplished to date. Many feel confident that this is a sound direction for our country, as evidenced by a 1991 Gallup Poll in which 64% of those surveyed believed that successful schools should be awarded more state and federal funds. Some, particularly the strong choice advocates, believe that attracting students will bring the additional funding necessary to provide financial incentives. The National Education Association is still quite cool to either individual or school rewards, especially if they involve competition, while the American Federation of Teachers strongly advocates the group reward concept. Dialogue over rewards is strongly linked to the debate over student testing profiled earlier in this chapter.

Sanctions

At the other end of the continuum, the notion of sanctioning groups and/or individuals for poor educational outcomes continues to be discussed and implemented across the nation. Referred to as "academic bankruptcy," at least 14 states have recently adopted formal provisions allowing state intervention if school districts fail to comply with specific requirements or attain certain outcomes. State provisions range from requiring the district to implement corrective action plans to a complete state takeover of the district, including the unseating of the local governing board. Frequently, the first step is the development of school district improvement plans and the allocation of additional state financial assistance in terms of personnel, training, and/or money. Districts then have one year or more to correct the deficiencies prior to further sanctions. Although some believe that market forces should allow these schools to go out of business, equity concerns for the students in the district have driven states to instead provide additional support. The public also feels strongly that funds should not be withdrawn from unsuccessful districts, as evidenced by a 1991 Gallup Poll showing only 33% believing that withdrawal of funds should be a sanction.

To date, only a few districts have actually been taken over, some initiated by the state, but at least one by the district itself. The Jersey City School District in New Jersey is perhaps the best known. The district had been under admonition from the state for nearly 5 years prior to the state takeover in 1989. Charges of abuse ranged from deplorable physical plants, to corrupt and inefficient fiscal practices, to employees who owed their jobs more to political connections than to talent. Indeed, the district's four high schools had more dropouts in 1987 than graduates. As part of the state takeover in 1989, the district's superintendent and the school board were replaced by a state-appointed superintendent and a 17-member advisory board. The new superintendent's reorganization of the central administration resulted in the reassignment, firing, or demotion of 117 central office personnel and a move toward school-site management (Olson, 1990b). New resources were acquired for building repairs and new programs. Critics challenge that the additional resources ($13 million) have made the difference, not the management changes. In Iowa, the State Board of Education seized control of the Hedrick Public Schools during November 1990, based on charges that the district had failed to provide minimum mandated academic offerings. During spring 1991 the district was "dissolved" by having its 230 students attend three adjoining districts. Critics charged that the takeover was the first step in a state effort to consolidate districts and destroy rural schools. Despite the charge, a U.S. District judge refused to halt the state's actions (Olson, 1990b).

As a final example, in July 1991 Rhode Island's Central Falls School District governing board requested the state to take over the district due to financial difficulties. Because the city of Central Falls was unable to adequately fund the district, the state provided additional funding, but it also appointed an administrator to oversee the district for at least the next school year (Diegmueller, 1991a).

State takeovers to date have focused primarily on fiscal issues, not necessarily academic ones. This is due to the lack of sound academic outcome data. Many states are frantically developing new assessment instruments and standardizing definitions of common indicators such as dropout and graduation rates. However, critics note that these provisions represent yet another state bureaucratic activity and that parental choice can accomplish the same results. Advocates indicate the key goal of these state takeovers is to ensure that appropriate education is available to students remaining in the school district. Policymakers frequently do not know the right thing to do, but know that corrective actions must be taken.

Kentucky—One Model

Incorporating many of the ideas related to rewards and sanctions, a comprehensive system was envisioned as part of Kentucky's Education Reform Act of 1990. Using a formula being created by the Kentucky State Board of Education, schools that have an increase of at least 1% in the proportion of successful students, including at-risk students, above their established threshold will receive financial rewards. The amount of the reward will be determined by applying the percentage set by the legislature to salaries of each certified staff person employed in the schools. By majority rule, the school staff will collectively decide how to utilize the reward funds. Different thresholds will be established for each school, depending upon baseline data. It is envisioned that bonuses could be as much as 1% for every 1% gain above the school's threshold.

On the other hand, schools that either fail to show improvement or decline will face consequences. Schools that show *no growth* in student achievement will be required to develop an improvement plan and are eligible for special state grants. If no improvements are made after 2 years, the school is assigned a Kentucky "Distinguished Educator," who has the authority to make extensive changes in school operations. These educators are to represent the state's most outstanding and highly skilled educators and are to take on the responsibility of working with less successful schools. Failure to improve after the third biennial assessment will result in the school's being declared a "school in crisis."

A school that experiences a *decline of up to 5%* must also develop a school improvement plan, is eligible for school improvement grants, and will have one or more distinguished educators assigned to the school, with the power to make changes. If improvements have not occurred after 2 years, the school is declared a "school in crisis." Any school that experiences a *decline of 5% or more* in any single 2-year period will immediately be declared a "school in crisis."

Being declared a "school in crisis" means all certificated staff are placed on probation; parents are given the right to transfer children to a successful school within the district or, if none exist, to one outside the district; personnel may be reduced or transferred if decline in student enrollment causes overstaffing; and the distinguished educator makes binding decisions regarding the retention, dismissal, or transfer of school staff. Evaluations are conducted every 6 months until the school is no longer in crisis.

These same rewards and sanctions apply to school districts as a whole. Central office staff are eligible for rewards if the entire district is successful, or the superintendent and school board are subject to dismissal if the entire district is declared to be in crisis. The first assessment cycle is slated to begin during 1993-1994, and nearly $30 million has been allotted for the development of performance-based assessments. In addition, an Office of Educational Accountability has been created as an independent arm of the legislature to monitor the education system and the implementation of the Education Reform Act. As one can imagine, a great deal of frantic activity is occurring throughout Kentucky.

Student/Parent Rewards and Sanctions

This section highlights several recent endeavors by educators and policymakers to hold students, as well as parents, responsible for learning outcomes. Many schools have used student, parent, and teacher contracts, but real consequences did not exist for those who failed to fulfill their side of the bargain. Instead, current activities carry significant consequences. As noted earlier, education is not viewed as a right under the federal constitution, nor under many state constitutions; instead, it is a privilege granted to people free of charge for a certain period of their lives, notwithstanding compulsory attendance laws requiring them to take advantage of this privilege up to a certain age (16 in most states). Therefore, many policymakers have looked for incentives for students to stay in school and perhaps continue into higher education. These activities are extremely controversial and many have been tested in court. However, to date, these actions have been upheld as not violating the rights of students or parents.

No Pass/No Play; No Attend/No Drive

During the mid-1980s, at least 14 states required students to maintain a certain grade average in order to participate in extracurricular sports and other club activities. In many cases, individual districts already had in place academic eligibility rules; however, the new state rules frequently strengthened the grade requirements. Initially, there was a great deal of concern over whether these rules would cause more students to drop out of school since sports and/or clubs may have been the reason they were still in school. Cries of inequity were made, claiming that these rules may have more adversely affected minority students. Indeed, after a few years, the results of these programs were clearly mixed. Limited research illustrates that the worst-case scenario of additional students dropping out did not occur, nor did student achievement necessarily improve. For example, only 38% of the Arizona school administrators responding to a 1990 department of education study indicated that the no pass/no play rule had helped to improve achievement; 62% noted that the situation was about the same.

More recent and perhaps more radical approaches to keeping students in school are the "no attend/no drive" or "no pass/no drive" regulations adopted by 12 states as of 1990. Similar but more intense equity challenges were made as these issues were enacted. Taking away a student's "right" to drive is extreme. On the other hand, so is the national dropout rate of nearly 30%. Gallup Poll data show that 62% of the respondents favor such programs. A brief review of provisions in two states follows.

West Virginia's 1988 "no attend/no drive" law was the first of its kind in the nation. It requires that when a high school student under 18 years of age misses 10 consecutive days without an acceptable excuse, or a total of 15 unexcused days in one semester, the school attendance officer must notify the Motor Vehicle Department. This department sends a notice of license suspension to the student, and if the license is not surrendered by the 30th day following notification, a police officer is sent to pick it up. To qualify for reissuance of the license, the student must pay a $15 fee and fulfill a probationary attendance period determined by the individual county, usually from 4 weeks to one semester.

Evaluation of program outcomes is mixed. Prior to the program, the state had a dropout rate of 17.4%; by 1990, the rate had dropped to 16.5%. However, of nearly 4,000 students surveyed, less than half (43%) of the students who had seriously thought about dropping out of school indicated that this law would keep them in school. Of those who dropped out and returned, only 12% stated it was because of the law. The general conclusion from this study was that the law is somewhat effective, but perhaps not as effective as had been hoped.

Florida's 1989 law suspends the licenses of students who have dropped out and those who have failing grades. As a result, Dade County, Florida, had suspended 10,000 licenses during the first 6 months of its program. Some school officials contend that the law should be repealed since it has resulted in tremendous paperwork burdens and also because students who are forced to leave school outnumber those who leave by choice. One administrator stated: "Until we start addressing [societal] failure, we deceive ourselves with public relations gimmicks that have no real connection with the problem, and do a disservice to our young people" (American Political Network, Inc., 1992e).

Parent Sanctions; "No Attend/No Welfare"

States and districts are also taking steps to make parents more responsible for their children's education. For example, during November 1990, the first parents were convicted as part of a stepped-up anti-truancy program in the Chicago Public Schools. These parents were sentenced to a year of court supervision and were told they could be jailed for up to 30 days and fined up to $500 under Illinois law if their 15-year-old child accumulated any more unexcused absences. This student had missed 80 of the mandatory 180 days during the previous school year, and 18 days of the current semester. Repeated warnings and offers of assistance had gone unheeded by the parents, according to school personnel. Results show that attendance in the district had improved to nearly 90%, compared to 74% prior to the new anti-truancy programs ("First parents," 1990).

Launched in 1988 by the Wisconsin legislature, *Learnfare* represents an effort to improve school attendance and high school completion by teenagers whose families are on welfare. Under this program, welfare families are subject to reduction of benefits when teenagers have more than two unexcused absences from school a month. The deduction for a family of four receiving a monthly grant of $617 would be about $100 (Cohen, 1992a). This controversial law was initially challenged in court, where a federal judge suspended the program in the Milwaukee schools for 4 months in 1990 until more accurate attendance records could be established. However, from that time, the program has been operating and more than 7,000 families' welfare checks have been reduced because their children skipped school.

Program critics state that many parents, on welfare or not, no longer have the ability to control the actions of their teenage children. One child can cause the loss of food on the table for the rest of the family. In addition, lawyers from the Legal Action of Wisconsin argue that the state spends too much money on attendance verification and welfare deduction paperwork. They indicate that this money should be spent to improve educational conditions within the inner cities. Supporters of the program indicate that parents have a responsibility to oversee the behavior of their children, and the state has a right to withhold assistance if this is not accomplished.

During early 1992, the first outside evaluation of *Learnfare* concluded that the program had not significantly improved the attendance among students whose families are on welfare. The study showed that only one-third of the students had improved attendance, while more than half had poorer attendance. Graduation rates for the *Learnfare* students were about the same as those of a control group of former welfare teenagers. In contrast, many program supporters claim that the overall tone of the report is negative, despite the possibility of positive interpretation. For example, the fact that these students are graduating at the same rate as the control group is good, and for one-third to have improved attendance is even better. They cite methodological errors and call the report biased from a liberal perspective.

A similar program for teenage parents is operating in Ohio, with discussions under way in many other states. Even more controversial is a new generation of proposals being developed across the nation that connect welfare payments not only to school attendance, but also to childbearing, health care, living arrangements, and marriage. During early 1992 New Jersey was the first state to actually enact a law establishing stricter work and education standards, providing new funds for job training and child care, eliminating disincentives for welfare mothers to marry so couples may remain together, and eliminating an increase in benefits when a welfare mother gives birth to an additional child (Cohen, 1992b). Proponents indicate that the aim of this "new paternalism" is to break the cycle of welfare dependency and to reinforce such values as school, work, marriage, and responsibility. Critics call the law "social engineering" and indicate that it will harm already struggling families, compel women to have abortions, and bury innocent children deeper into poverty. They are also concerned that these programs promote a view that welfare recipients are very different from everyone else, that they are not interested in health care, family stability, or good education.

The New Jersey program is merely part of a national movement to break the cycle of dependence by altering behaviors deemed counterproductive to both the individual and society. In Maryland, pending federal approval, welfare families would face substantial cuts in benefits unless they could show they were getting preventative health care, keeping their children in school, and paying their rent (Cohen, 1991). In California, a potential fall 1992 ballot initiative would provide financial incentives for welfare recipients to marry and would limit or cut benefits for additional children. Advocates of these activities believe that government ought to have certain expectations of those receiving public welfare benefits. Critics challenge that these provisions are based on the fallacy that people are primarily moved by economic calculations and hence can be controlled by altering financial incentives (Will, 1992). Nonetheless, supported by a blend of conservatives and liberals who are casting a cold eye on traditional notions of government compassion for the poor, this new paternalism is part of an accountability wave sweeping across the country.

Student Scholarships

On a more positive note, several states are moving ahead with student reward programs that are much more than simple recognition and plaques for outstanding achievement. As of spring 1991, at least nine states have implemented "guaranteed tuition assistance" programs for students who excel academically and meet certain income eligibility criteria. These programs carry inspiring names such as the *Rhode Island Children's Crusade for Higher Education,* the *New Mexico Scholars Program,* the *Maryland Educational Excellence Award Program,* and *Indiana's Twenty-First Century Scholars.* The general idea is for all students to realize that if they do well in school and want to go on to higher education or training, then economic conditions will not prevent them from doing so. In Rhode Island, the program is viewed as the most important economic development activity for the state.

Although the criteria vary slightly, in most states a student must demonstrate academic excellence by having a certain grade point average, graduating in the top portion of his or her class, or obtaining a certain score on the SAT or ACT. In addition, the student must come from a low-income family to receive full tuition support; students from middle-income families can receive partial tuition support. Some states allow support to be used only at in-state public community colleges or universities, while others allow students to choose from private colleges or training schools. As an example, the Arkansas Academic Challenge Scholarship will provide scholarships of up to $1,000 per year to any student who completes the following: takes the core curriculum and graduates from high school with at least a 3.0 GPA; scores 19 or above on the ACT; stays off drugs; enrolls in any Arkansas 4-year college or university; and has a family income of $30,000 or less for families with one child, with an extra $5,000 of income allowed per additional child (Jalomo & Bierlein, 1991a).

Most of these programs reach down into the lower elementary grade levels, whereas current scholarship programs do not make students aware of their existence until the final years in high school. By this time many of the highest at-risk students have already dropped out of the system physically and/or mentally. Overall, these programs represent a significant financial commitment on behalf of the state, yet preliminary qualitative outcome data are promising. Universal access to higher education within the United States is one more step closer to reality.

Educational Warranties

In addition to setting high standards, implementing new types of assessment systems, and providing real consequences, several states and many individual school districts are seeking to restore public and business confidence by issuing "warranties" on their graduates. Although the exact provisions vary, these warranties allow an employer to send a student back to high school for remediation if certain basic skills are lacking. Some districts guarantee only the student's basic ability to read, write, and perform mathematical calculations. Others have created explicit checklists of skills, including mastery of computer technology and team problem-solving. The Los Angeles School District plans to use a detailed set of job competencies identified by the U.S. Labor Secretary's Commission on Achieving Necessary Skills (Sommerfeld, 1992). To date, only Colorado and West Virginia require their districts to offer warranties, while Los Angeles Unified is the largest district following the trend. The New York City system will decide whether to fall in line by the end of school year 1992.

A similar concept offers a "certificate of employability" that speaks to a student's punctuality, positive work ethic, and ability to adapt to changing technology. In one Illinois district, students must complete 24 academic courses, cannot be absent more than an average of 6 days per year, and must attain certain attitude rankings in every course (e.g., promptness, effort, honesty, cooperation, responsibility, quality of work, initiative) in order to receive such a certificate. Of the first class of eligible students, 36% qualified for the certificate. Recent graduates believe that the certificate helped them gain employment.

Although these systems have existed since the late 1980s, few redemptions have occurred. For example, Prince George's County schools in Maryland have certified more than 9,000 graduates to date and have received only two complaints. Critics challenge these provisions are primarily publicity stunts and say that adequate resources are not available to accomplish the task. Proponents, including some teachers who consider these programs a vote of confidence, believe warranties will help build better relationships between education and industry and help students realize that their efforts in school make a difference. In addition, the programs put greater responsibility on teachers and administrators to avoid simply passing students through the system. Other states are considering adopting similar programs. Georgia's proposal would allow colleges to return students for remedial support, thereby eliminating the need for higher education remedial programs (American Political Network, Inc., 1992c).

Can Accountability Be Achieved?

This chapter has presented a broad array of activities and concepts under the umbrella term of *accountability,* including the establishment of goals, standards, assessments, rewards, and sanctions. As the public demands more information about educational outcomes and insists on consequences for those outcomes, many debates and issues have arisen. The first concern addresses the issue of whether Americans can decide what their expectations are for schools. It is difficult to hold someone accountable for general notions such as "a well-educated citizen." What does one actually need to know to be considered well educated? Many believe that in our pluralist society, reaching agreement on this issue will be very difficult if not impossible—and perhaps not even in the best interests of a democratic nation. Our forefathers purposely made education the responsibility of the states, not the federal government. A national curriculum and/or test would lead us in a direction they consciously avoided. However, many believe that without the establishment of some common goals, true equity of educational outcomes, not just access, cannot occur. This debate will continue for some time.

Educational testing that becomes too high-stakes elicits many concerns since assessment is not a "science." It is impossible to develop bias-free mental measurements; historically, the misuse of test data for student tracking, special education placement, and the watering down of curriculum has caused great damage. On the other hand, educators have dragged their feet on developing better assessment procedures and instruments. Many now believe that the new generation of performance-based testing, coupled with technological advances, will provide the accountability data desired while minimizing potential harm to students. Completion of such assessments, however, is several years away at best. Politics and the crises at hand are driving policymakers to act quickly, while outside pressures are keeping the momentum alive. The bottom-line question is whether higher standards and higher stakes testing for all students will indeed ensure equal educational opportunities for all students. The critics agree in theory, but disagree using pragmatic arguments based on time and money. Advocates indicate we will never know until we try, and that things cannot get much worse for, among others, our inner-city youths.

Finally, rewards and sanctions are becoming an integral part of accountability systems. Some note these government controls are unnecessary since rewards and sanctions will occur naturally as part of a parent choice system. Others note education is a public good that must receive some government protection as well as incentives. To this end, state takeovers are occurring, welfare families' benefits are decreasing, and students are losing driving privileges. But, students are also receiving higher education scholarships, and teachers and schools are receiving financial bonuses.

Will high uniform standards, sound performance-based assessment systems, and appropriate consequences help bring the United States back to the top of the international market? Few believe that these steps alone will accomplish this task, but they are essential ingredients. Others maintain that this drive for excellence through high-stakes accountability systems will greatly damage the strides made to date toward equity. The tension between excellence and equity continues.

5

What's the Big Deal About Choice?

Introduction

Perhaps one of the most controversial current educational policy debates involves that of educational choice. Listed by *Governing* as one of the top 10 legislative issues to watch during 1992, the concept continues to gain momentum (Katz, 1992). Generally, the thought is that parents should have the liberty to choose any public or private school for their children, with state funding supporting all or a portion of the costs. Since public schools can be viewed as a monopoly, many feel that introducing competition will serve as a powerful reform incentive toward excellence. Parents who currently cannot afford to pay tuition charges have no option but to send their children to neighborhood schools. As former Secretary of Education Lauro F. Cavazos noted in 1989:

> Some may disagree on the best way to give parents more options to choose from, and on how choice programs can be used to build better schools. But the jury is already in on this one: choice will be a critical element in education reform for years to come. Indeed, it may prove to be the linchpin in our common efforts to ensure all Americans—black and white, rich and poor, Asian and Native Americans, Hispanics, and the handicapped—have access to a quality education. (p. 8)

The principles of equity, efficiency, liberty, and excellence are readily visible within this debate. Underlying the arguments in favor of choice is the concept that all children should have access to excellent schools as chosen by their parents. The quality of their education should not be based upon their family's ability to live in a more affluent neighborhood; and, by providing access to all schools, greater equity can be achieved. Efficiency is instrumental because competition will force many schools to improve their operations. Excellence will be the net outcome since only the best schools would remain in business.

Critics also use these same principles to make their points. The notion of equity is undermined by the difficulties of providing adequate transportation for all students to attend their choice of school, and by the unequal financing of our schools. Many believe that establishing a system whereby already underfunded districts lose students does little to support efforts on their part to improve. Finally, many believe that the selection of schools will be based on *perceived* excellence rather than real excellence. Until better measures of outcomes are established, in addition to the parent training necessary to understand these assessments, choices will be made based on many factors other than excellence.

This chapter will examine the issue of choice in detail. General arguments will be broadened, and information relative to actual practice will be illustrated. The debate is emotional and grounded in few facts. The goal is to provide the reader with key philosophical arguments as well as empirical data regarding educational entities already implementing some dimension of a choice system.

Choice Defined

Before examining the debate, several definitions are necessary. *Public school choice* commonly refers to a system that allows school students to attend any public district or school within their state, regardless of their geographic residence. Currently, most students must attend a school within a specific attendance area of their resident district. Although many states allow student transfers at the discretion of local districts, the charging of tuition is fairly common when a parent wishes to enroll a child outside the district of residence. Under public school choice, parents would no longer be charged tuition to attend another district. Depending on capacity, districts or schools would be required to accept all resident students, followed by all nonresident pupils who wish to attend. As a synonymous term, *open enrollment* was used throughout the 1980s, although public school choice has now become the term of preference.

Within a public school choice system, two types of transfers are possible. *Intradistrict* enrollment allows the parent to seek enrollment in another school within the same district. *Interdistrict* enrollment allows the parent to seek enrollment in another district. A comprehensive public school choice system would allow both intradistrict and interdistrict options.

A broader concept of public school choice implies that parents will have several diverse options for the schooling of their children. These may include the opportunity to move between public schools, to dually enroll in postsecondary education institutions, or to select from a broad array of *magnet schools,* which emphasize specific subjects or modes of instruction (e.g., science, fine arts, the basics).

Finally, *private school choice* is the term used when the system allows parents to select from among public or private schools. A *voucher* is a mechanism whereby parents would receive a certificate worth a certain dollar amount when redeemed at a school of their choice. *Tuition tax credits* represent an alternative funding method in that parents would continue to pay tuition to the private school, but would receive a tax credit for all or some of the tuition charges.

The plethora of similar terms adds to a misunderstanding of not only the various programs being initiated across the country but also what outcomes these programs have achieved. For example, student achievement gains that followed the implementation of School District 4's choice program in Harlem (New York City) are frequently used as evidence to support statewide choice programs. However, District 4's program actually involves the development of magnet schools within a single school district. Individual schools, not districts across the state, are competing for students. Student transportation is not an issue because the district encompasses only one square mile within New York City, and several schools are located within the same building (Lieberman, 1990). These circumstances are very different from a statewide system. This example is offered not to pass judgment on District 4's program, but to illustrate how this debate involves concepts and terms not always interchangeable. Caution is urged to carefully understand the details before taking a stand.

In this chapter, three key terms will be used. *Public school choice* will be used when referring specifically to movement within or between the public school system. *Private school choice* will be used when referring to the inclusion of private schools. *Choice* will be used when discussing the more general philosophical issues of either system. Due to space limitations and their general acceptance, other options (e.g., magnet schools, postsecondary enrollment) will not be specifically addressed.

Historical Review

As with other controversial educational issues, roots of the choice debate can be tracked over time. Kirkpatrick (1990) traces the notion of competition and vouchers to Adam Smith's *Wealth of Nations* in 1776 and Thomas Paine's *The Rights of Man* in 1792. More than two centuries ago, Smith voiced concerns about teachers being public employees rather than educational entrepreneurs. He believed that anyone paid from the public purse, including teachers, lacked the motivation for performance possessed by those in the private realm. Therefore, some means to introduce competition into the system was essential. Paine took this idea one step further by proposing that England provide each pupil with an education allowance good for 6 years at any school of choice. His theory was that educational choice would promote competition and lead to the success and profitability of the best schools. Similar ideas arose in France during the 1880s and again in England during the 1920s. Specific actions were later taken in France in 1959 and in England in 1988 to operationalize these concepts.

The contemporary debate over choice was initiated in the United States by Milton Friedman in his 1955 book, *Economics and the Public Interest* (Underwood, 1991; Witte, 1991a). As a method of introducing free market forces into the educational system, Friedman advocated a system in which parents would receive tuition vouchers. Writers at that time offered the Servicemen's Readjustment Act of 1944 (the G.I. Bill) as an example. Under this act, millions of Americans received public monies to attend public and private institutions, including proprietary schools as well as seminaries and other religious schools. Kirkpatrick (1990) notes that few questions were raised about the constitutionality, the separation of church and state, or whether this freedom of choice was anything but a benefit to the individuals involved.

In 1970 the U.S. Office of Economic Opportunity released a report calling for implementation of a "regulated compensatory voucher," one that provided more money for students with special needs but did not allow parents to add money to the value of the voucher. Although the original goal was to include both public and private schools in the experiment, not only was recruiting school districts difficult, but state law restrictions were also found. These concerns reduced the pilot to one of intradistrict options within a single public school district: Alum Rock in California (Levin, 1991a). This 5-year pilot began in 1972.

Nationally, debate over the issue grew as word of the pilot program spread. Numerous editorials and comments both pro and con were generated. For example, in 1970, Robert Havighurst wrote: "While the educational Establishment slogs along, trying to do things a little better here and a little better there, the critics and the discontented demand drastic reforms. This is fertile soil for the idea of giving parents public money to find better schools for their children" (p. 52).

Surveys conducted in 1970 show that 43% of the general public as well as school administrators initially supported the choice concept. However, by 1971, support among school administrators was reduced by more than half to only 20%. Some believe this was due to educational associations' outcry against a voucher system. For example, at its annual meeting in 1970, the National Education Association (NEA) adopted a resolution stating that voucher plans could lead to racial, economic, and social isolation of children and would weaken or destroy the public school system. NEA urged that federal and state legislation be enacted to prohibit such plans (Kirkpatrick, 1990). Many advocates hastened to point out that this condemnation occurred prior to the implementation and evaluation of the pilot project. This information illustrates that today's debate is almost identical to the debate held more than 20 years ago. What happened during that time?

Evaluation of the Alum Rock pilot found widespread experimentation as 45 specialty programs or mini-schools were developed within 13 schools. In some cases, changes were quite radical, including flexible grade-level programs and open classrooms. School-level autonomy increased for both teachers and administrators. Parents were also found to take more interest in their child's education. Chaos, segregation, brutal competition, and other harmful results predicted by voucher critics did not occur. On the other hand, the studies generally found no impact on student achievement (Witte, 1991a). It should be noted, however, that this pilot was basically a magnet school program within a single district, *not* a full-fledged voucher system, as parents could not use their vouchers beyond the district.

In 1977, the 5-year Alum Rock project came to an end. Although the mini-schools were viewed with great excitement, they were discarded by the district during the final year of the project. In addition, the Alum Rock school board choose not to assume the additional costs the federal grant had absorbed during the pilot. Many critics of choice viewed this as a failed experiment. Others stated that change in leadership and political pressure led to its demise.

During the late 1970s and early 1980s, choice advocates continued their campaign. Authors such as John Coons noted that in other government-provided services, such as public housing, charity hospitals, and food programs, individual choice is not restricted as it is for K-12 education. Coons and others used these arguments to lobby for a constitutional initiative allowing vouchers within California (Levin, 1991a). There were not enough signatures gathered, however, to place the measure on the ballot.

In the early 1980s President Reagan advocated a system of tuition tax credits, whereby parents could deduct all or a portion of their tuition costs from their taxes. In addition, his administration unsuccessfully attempted in both 1983 and 1985 to convert the federal funding for disadvantaged students into individual vouchers. It was believed unfair for private school parents to pay twice, once for tuition and again in taxes. Proponents also felt that choice would force schools to either improve or go out of business. This type of rationale coming from a Republican president caused choice to be labeled a conservative idea, one that benefits the wealthy more than the poor. As a result, opposition was strong in both Congress and among educational organizations. Soon the momentum for parent voucher programs and/or tuition tax credits began to die down. By March 1983 John Coons wrote: "All signs are that the systems are comfortably ossified . . . I have to concede that the unions and the managers are a formidable force in favor of the status quo" (Kirkpatrick, 1990, p. 133).

Choice Activities During the Past Decade

A different type of momentum began during the mid-1980s. As the nation was told it was at risk because of its mediocre educational system, several states posed creative choices for parents. Significant differences from the past debate are evident. First, these ideas were initially limited to public schools, thereby silencing those opposed to the inclusion of the private sector. Second, individual states, not the federal government, took the lead; and third, new terms were coined such as *open enrollment* and *parental choice*. The state political debates, however, were no less lively than those at the federal level, focusing on the funding disparities among districts and the logistics of implementing statewide plans.

Minnesota was the first state to make the headlines. Supported by Governor Rudy Perpich, the state's multifaceted plan began in 1985 by allowing concurrent enrollment in postsecondary education institutions. Since that point, additional provisions include transfers between public schools and the establishment of charter schools. A landslide of state activity soon occurred; by spring 1991 formal public school choice legislation had been enacted in 9 states and bills introduced in at least 25. In some states, the legislation passed its first year with only minor difficulty; in others, several years of debate preceded implementation. However, the radical reform impact that some advocates had hoped for did not transpire.

A new book by researchers John Chubb and Terry Moe (1990), *Politics, Markets, and America's Schools,* revitalized interest regarding the inclusion of private schools in a state choice system. Chubb and Moe integrated the concept of decentralization in their reform proposal by stating that a system of choice will not work unless public schooling is greatly deregulated similar to private schools. Conservative think tanks and newspaper editorialists worked hard to spread these ideas, but they were also careful not to use old terms, such as *voucher system* or *tuition tax credits.*

Wisconsin was next to make the headlines. In 1990 there was legislation enacted that allowed a small percentage of low-income students within the Milwaukee Public Schools to attend private nonsectarian schools. Annette ("Polly") Williams, a black legislator from Milwaukee, viewed her initiative as a means to provide quality education for poor students trapped within the city's public school system. Not unexpectedly, this controversial program was immediately challenged in court.

Advancement of choice in Wisconsin, however, did not necessarily indicate that the tide had turned. In fall 1990 voters in Oregon strongly rejected a ballot initiative that would have established both interdistrict public school choice and a tax credit of up to $2,500 for private school tuition or home instruction. Defeat of this measure was due to an effective lobbying campaign by opponents, including the teacher unions (Finn, 1991).

What will the future bring? President Bush's *America 2000: An Education Strategy* (1991) recommends private school choice as one of 15 elements in its accountability section. As of spring 1992, 32 states had declared themselves *America 2000* states and vowed to implement strategies to meet the national goals. Although strong opposition remains, legislative efforts or citizen initiatives to implement private school choice continue across the nation. While reform experts initially predicted that private school choice would never occur because of political pressure, these same people are now less skeptical because the current momentum is coming from the states.

This brief historical sketch illustrates how controversial educational policy debates follow cyclical patterns over time. An idea first conceptualized more than 200 years ago is again at the forefront of the policy debate. Newspaper clippings from 1970 on choice closely resemble those in 1992. Since this issue is destined to remain central to educational reform for some years to come, a closer examination of the debate follows.

Specific Choice Programs

Table 5.1 lists the nine states that had adopted some type of formal public school interdistrict and/or intradistrict choice system as of spring 1991. It also identifies Wisconsin as the only state to have implemented a private choice plan. Overall, most states have implemented voluntary-type programs. Only four (Iowa, Minnesota, Colorado, and Ohio) have mandatory interdistrict public school choice provisions, whereby districts must allow students to leave and must accept other students if capacity exists. Others encourage student transfers through voluntary participation of districts, with Colorado funding magnet schools within several districts that were willing to try interdistrict transfers. A few state programs are fairly restrictive, such as in Ohio, where students can transfer only to an adjacent district, and in Washington, where parents can still be charged a transfer fee (i.e., tuition). Considering that public and/or private school choice legislation has been introduced in the majority of states, the limited number of comprehensive programs illustrates the intensity of the debate and the strength of the opposition.

Table 5.1 States With Formal Choice Statutory Provisions as of Spring 1991

State	Intradistrict		Interdistrict		Private Schools	
Arkansas	V	(existing)	V	('89/90)		
Colorado	M	('90/91)	V pilot	('90/91)		
Idaho	V	(existing)	V	('91/92)		
Iowa	V	('89/90)	M	('89/90)		
Minnesota	V	(existing)	M	('90/91)		
Nebraska	V	(existing)	M	('93/94)		
Ohio	M	('93/94)	V	('93/94)		
Utah	V	('90/91)	V	('90/91)		
Washington	V	('90/91)	M	('90/91)		
Wisconsin (Milwaukee School District only)					M	('90/91)

V = Voluntary: districts may choose to participate
M = Mandatory: districts are required to participate

Several other states have "informal" choice provisions, whereby their existing statutes have allowed student transfers for many years. For example, Arizona permits both intra- and interdistrict movement at the discretion of districts, while Vermont enables students in a district lacking an elementary and/or high school to be tuitioned to a public or a state-approved nonsectarian private school. Alabama permits intradistrict "schools of choice" that promote choice among educational programs. Oregon has a limited program for students who require additional support, as determined through a new state assessment system, while Kentucky allows students to transfer in the event their school is declared "in crisis."

This represents a general overview of state activity related to student transfers within and between districts. For more detail, profiles of two state programs follow.

Minnesota: Considered the leading state in the choice movement, Minnesota provides a variety of options to students. Initiated in 1984, the "Postsecondary Enrollment Option" allows public school 11th-grade and 12th-grade students to attend nonsectarian private or public colleges, universities, and vocational institutions. The state pays the tuition costs if the postsecondary credits are used primarily as high school credit; students desiring dual credit or those attending high school full-time while earning college credit must pay the tuition charges themselves. During 1990-1991, approximately 6,200 students (5% of all eligible students) participated in the program, and the component is viewed by some Minnesota policy experts as having the greatest impact on students. Following Minnesota's lead, a growing number of states have adopted similar postsecondary enrollment provisions (e.g., Ohio, Washington, Wisconsin, Arkansas).

Minnesota's "School District Enrollment Options Program" allows elementary and secondary students to attend the public school of their choice if capacity exists and desegregation provisions are not violated. This plan was initiated in 1987 and was phased in over 3 years to become mandatory for all districts in 1990. Parents are responsible for providing transportation to the border of the nonresident district, at which point the latter becomes responsible. During 1990 the state appropriated $50,000 to reimburse low-income parents for either all or a portion of their transportation costs. Districts are allowed to establish capacity limits for their schools or programs, and parents must meet certain application deadlines. Minnesota's state department of education has established an "800" telephone number, runs radio messages, and distributes brochures to inform parents of their options. In 1990 just slightly less than 1% of the students participated (approximately 3,200 of 730,000 students). This low participation rate is of interest since many choice advocates initially believed this provision would result in more radical changes.

Also initiated in 1987, Minnesota's third component—the "High School Graduation Incentives Program"—allows at-risk persons ages 12 to 21 to earn a high school diploma by choosing from various state-funded programs. These programs include enrolling in the public school of their choice or a private school that has contracted with the state to provide services, enrolling in state-approved public alternative education programs, attending an Area Learning Center, or attending courses at a college or technical school. Persons eligible for this program are those considered at risk, based on characteristics such as chronic truancy, dropping out, substance abuse, and teenage pregnancy.

Most recently, in 1991 the state authorized the establishment of up to eight outcome-based "charter schools," whereby any group of certificated teachers can seek approval to create their own school. These teachers must obtain sponsorship from a public district governing board and final approval from the state board of education. Each charter school must hold an election to establish a board of directors with the authority to hire/fire all personnel and make decisions regarding curriculum, budgeting, and school operations. These schools are exempt from most state laws and board rules, except those related to health and safety, certification, special education, due process, and financial audits. The school must be nonsectarian and cannot charge tuition beyond the state voucher amount.

The concept has generated a variety of teacher- and community-driven proposals, ranging from citizens hoping to save an elementary school, to a maverick teacher trying to create a multi-age alternative program within her district, to the St. Paul branch of the NAACP, which is considering applying for a charter to create a program providing educational and social services to entire families. U.S. Senator Dave Durenberger of Minnesota is attempting to obtain federal funds to help support initial planning costs for these programs (Olson, 1992a). Of plans submitted to date, a private Montessori school was the first charter school approved and will begin receiving state funding during 1992.

Although the state began with a public school choice system, the door was opened through the charter concept for private school involvement. While Minnesota's educational associations reluctantly endorsed the initial choice options, the Minnesota Federation of Teachers claims that the charter school law lacks sufficient collective-bargaining guarantees for teachers, puts existing schools at a disadvantage by not extending deregulation to all schools, and fails to ensure adequate accountability. Controversies over this topic continue.

A growing movement among states to enact similar legislation is occurring. As of January 1992, lawmakers in at least seven states—Arizona, California, Connecticut, Florida, Massachusetts, Michigan, and Tennessee—were either exploring or planning to introduce charter school legislation. Minnesota continues to be a choice leader for the country.

Wisconsin: In March 1990 the Wisconsin legislature enacted the "Milwaukee Parental Choice Program." Sponsored by Milwaukee legislator Polly Williams, the program allows up to 1% (approximately 1,000) of Milwaukee public school students who are low-income to attend private, nonsectarian schools and provides roughly $2,500 for each student. Private schools that wish to participate must be nonsectarian; have been in existence for at least one year; have a minimum of 51% of their students paying tuition; take all applicants if capacity exists (including special needs students); use a random selection lottery process if the number of applicants exceeds capacity; not charge additional tuition for the state voucher students; and follow existing general state statutes covering private schools (e.g., provide a minimum number of hours of instruction; offer a sequential curriculum in 13 subject areas) (Sheane & Bierlein, 1991).

Private schools participating in the programs must also meet one of the following standards for the pupils involved in the program: (a) at least 70% must advance one grade level each year; (b) pupils' average attendance rate is at least 90%; (c) at least 80% demonstrate significant academic progress; or (d) at least 70% of the families meet parent involvement criteria established by the private school (Underwood, 1991).

During 1990-1991, 10 private schools enrolled 341 choice students, of which 249 completed the school year. In February 1991 one of the private schools enrolling 63 students closed, causing most of these students to return to the public school system. During the second year of the program, 562 choice students enrolled, of whom 155 were students from the previous year. Of the 94 students who chose not to return, only 8 graduated. It is uncertain as to why such a large number choose not to return (Witte, 1991b).

Research on the program is being conducted by John Witte from the University of Wisconsin-Madison. His report on the program's first year reveals several interesting findings. On the positive side, the program did not skim off the best students, but instead appears to have provided an alternative educational environment for low-income students who were not succeeding in the public school system. In addition, student attendance, parental attitudes toward choice schools, and parental involvement were all positive. Indeed, 84% of the participating parents gave their new choice schools a grade of "A" or "B," whereas only 32% had given this rating to their previous public school. On the other hand, achievement scores did not increase, and attrition from the program was very high. Witte recommends several changes, including a requirement that choice schools have a formal governance structure, conduct annual financial audits, and meet all current and future state outcome requirements. He also recommends that the state provide additional program information to students, and that special education programming be addressed (i.e., the County Circuit Court found that the private choice schools must admit handicapped students but are not required to provide a program for them).

Ongoing hearings have occurred since the program's implementation. Initially, the Milwaukee branch of the NAACP, the Wisconsin Association of School District Administrators, and the Wisconsin Education Association filed an action against the program with the state's Supreme Court; however, the court refused to hear the action. Instead, a second action was filed with the Dane County Circuit Court by several parents and a number of private schools. This lower court declared the program constitutional, but the Wisconsin Court of Appeals determined that the program was unconstitutional due to procedural violations. In March 1992 the Wisconsin Supreme Court declared the program constitutional. Although this state court ruling impacts only the Wisconsin program, many states were waiting for this decision as a signal to move ahead with similar legislation.

Choice—An Idea With Lots of Appeal

The issue of choice serves to divide people into being either strong choice advocates or avid opponents; however, it has not become a purely Republican versus Democrat, or conservative versus liberal debate. Instead, the concept has some appeal to different groups for various reasons. For example, choice is very attractive to conservative thinkers, including Republican legislators and governors. They note that the existing "non-choice" educational system achieved little during the 1980s, despite significant additional resources. There is great appeal to shaking up the system without spending more than a small amount for additional transportation. In addition, these ideas have been strongly advocated by conservative policy analysts and by both the Reagan and Bush administrations.

The notion also appeals to some Democrats. Unlike tuition tax vouchers, many minority parents support the concept as a means to provide equal access for their children to the "better" schools, although most organizations, such as the NAACP, oppose the concept. The issue in Minnesota was successfully initiated by Governor Perpich and the state

Table 5.2 Public Opinion on Public and Private School Choice—Gallup Poll Percentages

	1970	1971	1981	1983	1985	1986	1987	1991
Favor	43	38	43	51	45	46	44	50
Oppose	46	44	41	38	40	41	41	39
Don't know	11	18	16	11	15	13	15	11

SOURCE: "The 23rd Annual Gallup Poll of the Public's Attitudes Toward the Public Schools" by S. M. Elam, L. C. Rose, & A. M. Gallup, *Phi Delta Kappan, 73*(1), p. 47, September 1991. Reprinted with permission. The question was: "In some nations, the government allocates a certain amount of money for each child's education. The parents can then send the child to any public, parochial, or private school they choose. This is called the 'voucher system.' Would you like to see such an idea adopted in this country?"

chief school officer, both Democrats. Representative Williams in Wisconsin, a Democrat, has become a powerful spokesperson for private school options for low-income inner-city students. As part of the 1992 presidential campaign, all five initial Democratic contenders stated their opposition to private school choice plans, but offered varying degrees of support for public school choice plans.

The general public appears to support both public and private choice concepts in their simplest forms. When asked if they believe parents should have the right to send their child to any school of choice utilizing state funds, their instincts for liberty encourage them to respond affirmatively. Table 5.2 illustrates the results of Gallup Poll data during the past two decades. Although supporters have never been in the majority, the 1991 poll illustrated that 50% of the respondents favored private vouchers, while 39% opposed them. This represented an increase of 6 percentage points since 1987.

However, many contend that few respondents understand the complexity of the issue and that the wording of the question makes a difference. For example, two recent Arizona polls illustrate that the outcome depends on how the question is presented. A poll commissioned by a pro-choice business group during October 1991 revealed that 54% of respondents affirmed the following question:

> Some people suggest the government allot a certain amount of money for each child's education. Parents can then send the child to any public, private, or parochial school they choose. This is called the voucher

system. Would you like to see such an idea adopted in this state? (ABLE Education Foundation, Inc., 1991)

A few weeks later, only 37% of the respondents in a poll conducted by a major Arizona newspaper responded favorably to a similar question: "Please tell me whether you favor or oppose . . . giving parents public funds to use in sending their children to the public, private or parochial school of their choice" (Pitzl, 1991). Policymakers relying on such data need to be keenly aware of how the survey question is worded.

During the initial push for public school choice, many corporate leaders and business organizations openly advocated for this reform. David Kearns (1988), then chairman and chief executive officer of the Xerox Corporation, stated the following:

> Today's public education system is a failed monopoly—bureaucratic, rigid and in unsteady control of dissatisfied captive markets. Competition for students and dollars would break that monopoly and reinvigorate the schools. . . . For the first time, operating income would be directly related to customer service. For the first time, poor families would have options enjoyed only by the affluent today. (p. 3)

However, it is important to note that Kearns' remarks were focused only on public school choice, and with few exceptions, most national business organizations involved in educational reform have not endorsed private school choice. Groups such as the Committee for Economic Development, the Business Roundtable, and the National Alliance of Business have made public school choice an integral part of their reform platforms, but neither as the sole panacea nor as the leading activity. As a result, these groups are the target of strong criticism from the Heritage Foundation, a Washington-based conservative think tank, for not challenging the political status quo (Weisman, 1991). In a similar vein, President Bush's *America 2000* platform *does* include private school choice, but again only as one element amidst many reforms.

Overall, the notion of providing additional options for parents and students appeals to many Americans. Consensus breaks down when the "how" is discussed. Conservative Republican policymakers embrace the hope that market forces will drive reform and want full private school choice with no strings attached. Moderates have a difficult time accepting choice as a panacea, but will accept public school choice and private school involvement if an equal playing field can be established. Some Democrats see it as a way to provide opportunities for those less fortunate, but the vast majority do not support public or private choice systems, partly in response to strong opposition from the educational organizations. They instead want additional funding to establish magnet programs.

Specific Aspects of the Debate

The resulting war is fought on several fronts. Advocates rely on philosophical democratic and market principles, while critics take a pragmatic approach, attacking the details (or lack thereof). Generally, advocates propose that liberty, or choice, is one of the major tenets of a democratic society. Families should have the right to choose the type of education they want for their children (Nathan, 1989b). Just as they have a right to raise their children with a particular set of traditions and values, they should be able to select a particular school or curriculum that will best meet their children's needs. Currently, parents can exercise this choice option by either moving their residence or paying tuition to a private school. Both of these options are limited for lower socioeconomic families; therefore, choice systems are necessary to provide equal liberties for all citizens.

A second general argument for choice is that it will lead to greater competition for students and improvements in school outcomes. The belief is that most schools have a monopoly over students in their attendance areas and therefore do not have competitive pressure to use resources efficiently (Levin, 1991a). This second argument is the one most debated by practitioners.

Unfortunately, little empirical evidence exists to support arguments offered by either side. Sketchy statutory language has not greatly affected programs within various states (i.e., the worst case scenario has not occurred), but dramatic reform and improvements have also not occurred (i.e., even the inclusion of private schools in the Milwaukee program has not improved student achievement). It is an issue along which lines are drawn and weapons sharpened. As noted by Hayes (1992), "Wouldn't it be funny if, after a few years of experiments with choice plans around the country, both sides, critics and advocates, turned out to be mostly wrong?" (p. 491). As an example, in Britain, where public school choice has been in operation since 1988, parents have found they have less choice than they want because good schools immediately fill up and bad schools sink slowly. Chira (1992) states: "Overall . . . choice [in Britain] appears to have had neither the catastrophic effects its critics feared nor the rejuvenating impact its advocates predicted" (p. A1). Until empirical data become available, conclusions should be drawn only after a careful examination of the debate. Additional details follow.

Equal Educational Opportunity/Access Issues

One of the greatest concerns launched by critics of choice is that a system cannot be developed that is truly equal for all students, particularly for those from low socioeconomic families. Several issues arise. One deals with the ability of parents to gain *access to information* and to use that information to make appropriate decisions for their children. Many note that some parents are well prepared by their education, experience, and access to information to make beneficial choices on behalf of their children, while other parents—especially those from groups already most disadvantaged by society—are left to "choose" between mediocre schools. This is especially true when lack of information, materials in appropriate languages, or assistance undermines their opportunities for selection. In response, choice advocates indicate that market forces will require schools to widely distribute information about their programs, and some choice plans call for the establishment of parent information centers (Chubb & Moe, 1990).

Critics also voice concern about "truth in advertising" issues and worry that the less-educated parents might fall prey to sham operations (Finch, 1989; George & Farrell, 1990). This concern is voiced particularly when private schools are included, since few state laws govern these schools. Even some choice advocates have acknowledged that "undoubtedly there will be fraudulent and dishonest school operators. Such people currently operate in almost every walk of life" (Rinehart & Lee, 1991, p. 157). Kirkpatrick (1990) acknowledges that "there will be mistakes; there may be schools that seem strange. But this is a price that must be paid if genius, creativity, and progress are to prosper" (p. 45). However, these authors indicate that under the G.I. Bill, these instances seldom occurred; active competition forced schools to protect their reputations. Some believe state minimums are necessary, but only for health, safety, and nondiscrimination (Lieberman, 1990).

Choice critics are concerned that parents will make judgments based on factors other than educational outcomes. For example, data collected on the Minnesota program during 1989-1990 illustrate that more than 40% of the reasons given for open enrollment transfers were "convenience-based" (ERS Research Digest, 1990). These included geographic proximity, day-care, parents working in another district, and plans to move into or out of the district. Twenty percent of the reasons were academic in nature, focusing on a desire for a specific program or greater academic opportunity. Six percent transferred for extracurricular, athletic, or social reasons. Critics use these findings to illustrate that educational excellence is not the key reason parents seek to transfer. For example, Finch (1989) points out that a group of Minnesota parents chose to transfer their children because the school board had voted to close down one of two high schools as part of a move to consolidate services. He claims that their motive was one of defiance and retaliation, not the improvement of education.

Advocates indicate that it really does not matter why parents want to move, as long as they feel more empowered and involved in the education of their child. Evidence extracted from a review of magnet school choice programs illustrates that students perform better and accomplish more in learning environments they have freely chosen than in those to which they are simply assigned (Raywid, 1989). Data collected on the Milwaukee private school experiment during 1990-1991 also supports this point of view. Survey results show that 89% of the program's parents believed that the educational quality in the chosen school was important, while 66% indicated that they were frustrated with the public schools (Witte, 1991a).

Another issue involves *adequate and appropriate transportation* to schools of choice. When financially strapped states were initially considering the implementation of an interdistrict public school choice plan, many believed it could be done without additional funding. However, concerns arose over how students from lower socioeconomic families would be able to transport themselves to a school of choice. For example, in Massachusetts, where no transportation assistance was provided, data reveal that only a very small percentage of low-income students took advantage of choice; 93% of participants were white, middle-class students (Diegmueller, 1991b).

Overall, however, most states with formal statewide public school choice provisions have allocated additional funds to provide transportation for low income students. To control costs, this transportation subsidy is limited to a maximum number of miles per week or to adjacent districts. Critics argue that these limitations prohibit rural students from accessing the schools in the city or suburbs, and recommend funding for boarding facilities. Choice advocates respond that transportation will not be an issue if private schools are allowed to participate, since new schools will be developed within communities where a market exists, including inner-city and rural areas (Rinehart & Lee, 1991). Taking existing transportation expenditures and creating individual student subsidies may also stimulate private, competitively priced transportation companies.

Fair and objective admissions criteria are also voiced as a major equity concern. Some fear that elitist schools will be established, whereby schools select only the best and brightest, or select students based on race or gender. Moore and Davenport (1989) analyzed the admissions criteria utilized as part of four major cities' magnet school programs (New York, Chicago, Boston, and Philadelphia). They found that "school choice has typically become a new improved method of student sorting, in which schools pick and choose among students" (p. 13).

Although Moore and Davenport focused on district magnet programs rather than statewide choice, their findings show that these programs typically admit high percentages of white students relative to their overall district enrollment. Conversely, percentages were very low for students who were handicapped or limited English proficient, and for students with a history of poor attendance and/or previous behavior problems. They attribute these findings to complex admission procedures best understood by middle-class families, admission criteria that required certain scores on tests and academic history, and limited programs that could accommodate handicapped or limited English proficient students. In addition, aggressive recruiting occurred at middle-class schools, while students in low-income schools received only a booklet advertising available options. Finally, teacher preferences for high-achieving students existed.

As a means of protection, most formal state choice provisions require nonresident students to be selected in a nondiscriminatory manner.

Many districts utilize, or are moving toward utilizing, a lottery system to avoid the first come, first served method of registering. Without this provision, unequal access is an issue since low-income parents do not have the same latitude to miss work while standing in line to register their children (Farrell, 1990). In reference to potential race or ethnic discrimination charges, advocates indicate that many protections are already built into the system through federal and state laws. Charges can be filed against those schools that adopt admission procedures resulting in discriminatory decisions. Indeed, having a formal state choice program with uniform guidelines would mitigate many current discriminatory activities.

Concerns are also voiced over allowing schools to require certain areas of expertise or skill for admittance (e.g., certain test scores for a gifted school, or a performing arts audition). Concern is diminished if every student is "guaranteed" enrollment in his or her resident school and if the selection criteria do not utilize discriminatory procedures (e.g., an assessment with known sex or gender bias). However, some choice advocates envision a system where every student would be required to seek enrollment in a school. No student would be guaranteed a place; if an adequate student funding weight is provided, competitive forces will provide an appropriate school for every child.

Finally, under the general category of equal access, many are concerned about *segregation issues*. Each current public school choice system allows districts under court order or an agreement with the Office of Civil Rights to prohibit student transfers if they would result in noncompliance. However, many borderline districts are concerned that slight population shifts could cause them to be "thrown into desegregation." States are also concerned because of the additional funding necessary to support the court-ordered compliance activities for these districts (e.g., busing, magnet schools). The Office of Civil Rights has indicated its support for choice by claiming segregation would not be at issue as long as deliberate discrimination is not the cause of racial imbalance. Choice advocates indicate that many public schools are presently highly segregated because of housing patterns; and, under a choice system, minorities would be given access out of presently segregated ghetto schools (Rinehart & Lee, 1991).

Lieberman (1990) points out that the major advocacy organizations for minorities have not supported public or private choice plans. He indicates that "neither the NAACP, the NAACP Legal Defense and

Education Fund or the Urban League has endorsed public school choice; the NAACP Legal Defense and Education Fund has been openly critical if not hostile to it" (p. 40). In addition, many inner-city minority communities are concerned that their best and brightest will seek enrollment outside their district. Instead of "white flight," people refer to the possibility of "brain drain." These communities are attempting to revitalize their neighborhoods and are concerned that efforts should be focused on supporting their schools, not offering their students a way out. In response, advocates indicate that the poor and disadvantaged have the most to gain since they currently have the least opportunity to change locations. Citing 1991 Gallup Poll data, they note that strongest support for private school choice came from nonwhites and blacks (57% support in both groups), inner-city dwellers (also 57%), people with children under 18 (58%), and nonpublic school parents (66% support). Choice advocates believe bureaucratic inertia is the explanation for resistance by major minority organizations.

Finance Issues

Although related to equal access issues described above, additional concerns about financing are voiced in the choice debate. The first focuses on an inadequate and inequitable financing system. As shown in Chapter 2, school districts do not have access to equal amounts per student, and only a few states provide additional funding to support the needs of economically disadvantaged students. Therefore, many inner-city districts are at a disadvantage entering the competition. Their facilities and extracurricular programs may not be as extensive because a larger portion of their budgets must be utilized for counselors, social service workers, and security.

Choice supporters indicate that adequate funding weights should be provided in order to make low-income and other special needs students attractive. However, current choice states do not provide additional funding for low-income students beyond transportation. To date, the funding disparity issue has been paramount during the debate, but not once actual implementation occurs, since so few students are actually transferring.

The debate intensifies, however, when the *costs of including private schools* are considered. Since states are not currently supporting the educational costs of private school students, providing a voucher for all students represents a major expense. For example, in Arizona, approximately 30,000 students are enrolled in private schools for which the state provides no financial support. If a full voucher system were implemented, these students would become eligible for state funding. Using an average cost of $4,000 per student, this equates to an additional $120 million. While this represents only a small percentage of the nearly $2 billion K-12 education budget, it would be large enough to provide preschool education for every low-income 3-year-old and 4-year-old in the state ($50 million) and fully fund the state's successful pilot career ladder system for teachers ($70 million). On the other hand, choice advocates state that private school competition will force decentralization of authority, and a great deal of funding can be recouped from less bureaucracy.

The financial implications of including private schools has caused some choice advocates to propose smaller voucher amounts (e.g., $600), which they indicate would be adequate to help many families cover private school tuition. However, student equity issues arise because only wealthier families could afford the additional tuition not supported by the voucher. Egalitarians have emphasized that an unregulated market would increase the expenditures of the rich more than those of the poor, further exacerbating present resource inequalities instead of reducing them (Farrell, 1990). Concerns like this have arisen in Vermont towns that offer a choice option when parents wishing to use their funding at a more costly school must make up the difference (Goldberg, 1988).

Other proposals, such as in the Milwaukee program, limit the voucher to low-income students previously enrolled in the public school system. Under this scenario, the state has already been paying for these students, and existing funds can be transferred. These provisions, however, greatly undermine the notion of a full voucher system. Considering that more than 5.5 million students are currently enrolled in private schools across the country, the total cost of implementing a full private school choice system would be at least $22 billion. Many claim that this money would be better used to support the ailing public school system. Others argue that money is not the answer, but rather reorganization as driven by parental liberty.

Other financial concerns center on *local funding issues*. Currently, states allow districts to raise additional revenues through governing board approval and/or local elections. If parents have chosen to send their child to a nonresident district, several questions arise. Should a portion of the local funding generated for that resident student be transferred to the new district of attendance and, if so, how can this be done fairly and with minimal administrative cost? Indeed, several states require that districts "bill" each other for portions of this additional revenue (e.g., Utah) or for high-cost special education students (e.g., Minnesota). Second, if funds are not transferred, will parents support efforts to raising additional local revenues for a district their child no longer attends? A new dimension of school financing issues has arisen.

One idea posed by Allan Odden, co-director of the Consortium for Policy Research in Education (CPRE) Finance Center, would require states to support the "base" funding for all districts. Any additional local revenues would be generated by an income surcharge imposed on those parents whose children attend the school. In the case where the school serves primarily low-income parents, the state or federal government would guarantee a per pupil yield (Odden, 1991). When discussed with several Arizona school and public finance experts, this idea was soundly rejected due to the complexity of redesigning a system that generated individual school revenue through an income tax on enrollees.

Finally, critics indicate that choice involves a *flawed rewards and sanctions system* that will not produce the improvements advocates want. First, if a "bad" school begins to lose students, it also immediately loses funds that could have been used for school improvement. For example, if a district loses 10 students at $4,000 per student, it has lost the equivalent funding of one teacher. However, the 10 students may have come from different classrooms, thereby not allowing a reduction of one teacher. Advocates say funding losses can be made up through decreases in administration, but fairly small districts argue that their overhead is minimal.

Critics also note that forcing districts out of business through a gradual loss of funding is detrimental for remaining students and is not reflective of sound business practices. Unlike private business, public school districts are not eligible to obtain bank loans for major school improvement efforts. In addition, critics have used the savings and loan and the Chrysler Corporation bailouts to illustrate that similar considerations should be given to failing districts. To minimize this concern, several states either included an initial phase-down of funding loss or delayed effective dates, giving districts time to improve. However, these provisions also cost states additional money in that they were "double funding" students during the phase-down.

Additionally, critics indicate that attracting new students is beneficial only up to a point. As long as the district has additional capacity, attracting new students is a financial boost. However, once capacity has been reached, the cost of securing additional building space becomes a disincentive to attracting more students. Advocates, however, cite this reasoning as typical of educators not "thinking outside the box" because schools of the future need not be contained within traditional buildings. Instead, leasing existing space in office complexes or utilizing other creative financing arrangements would be one outcome of competition. Critics counter that such privatization of schooling would dehumanize schools; students would be viewed only in terms of their monetary worth.

Common School/Constitutional Issues

Several arguments challenge that a private school choice system would *undermine the goals of America's common schools.* Schooling in this country has both private and public functions. As Levin (1991a) writes:

> It has long been established that schooling will ultimately enhance individuals' production and earnings, trainability, health, efficiency in consumption, access to information, and a wide variety of other private outcomes. . . . [However,] it is widely recognized that democratic and capitalist societies must rely heavily upon their schools to provide an education that will preserve and support the fundamental political, social, and economic institutions that comprise those societies . . . [and] contribute to equality of social, economic, and political opportunities among persons drawn from different racial and social class origins. (p. 139)

To this end, critics of private choice systems are concerned that competition will create specialized systems that no longer expose students to a common educational experience. Stemming from Horace Mann's call for a larger loyalty, there is some concern that a system of government-assisted private schools would be created, providing little opportunity for students to experience the diversity of backgrounds and viewpoints that contribute to the democratic process. Many believe that it would be unrealistic to expect Catholic schools to expose their students to both sides of the abortion issue, or military academies to debate the value of disarmament and peace movements. The curricula and faculty in these schools would be selected to make them efficient competitors in a differentiated market for students. This in turn would limit students' freedom of choice. Some believe that the state has a responsibility to provide children with a view of the world other than that of their parents (Kirst, 1984). The right of parents to choose experiences, influences, and values to which they expose their children conflicts with the right of a democratic society to use the educational system to inculcate certain economic, political, and social values.

There is also some concern that parental pedagogical preferences may continue social class differences. It has been shown that middle- and upper-class parents are more likely to choose child-centered instructional approaches that stress independence and critical thinking, while lower socioeconomic parents emphasize conformity and are more likely to choose schools utilizing conventional methods, such as drill and practice. This could have two major consequences. First, since socioeconomic status often parallels racial lines, parental choice of pedagogy may result in racial isolation (Lieberman, 1990). Second, future careers and salary earnings may depend on these choices. Most professional and managerial positions need individuals with good critical thinking skills, while jobs of low occupational levels stress a high degree of discipline, concentration on basic skills, and following orders.

Choice advocates indicate that the common school notion is more a myth than a reality because of current differences among public schools. What does not exist, however, is a mechanism for parents to choose from these alternatives. Instead, by virtue of residence (as determined by socioeconomic status), students attend schools that are a reflection of their community. Choice would provide more equitable educational opportunities for all children.

Finally, the fear of prolonged court cases over *separation of church and state* has kept most of the choice debate focused on only the inclusion of nonsectarian schools. Using the First Amendment, which specifies that Congress shall make no law promoting or prohibiting the free exercise of religion, state and federal courts have struck down repeated state efforts to provide direct subsidies to religious schools (Guthrie et al., 1988).

Since 1971 the U.S. Supreme Court has analyzed private school subsidy cases under tests articulated in *Lemon v. Kurtsman* as expanded in *Bowen v. Kendrick*. Specifically, the combined Lemon/Bowen test asks whether the statute: (a) has legitimate secular purpose; (b) does not have the primary effect of advancing religion; and (c) does not create "excessive entanglement" with religion via comprehensive and continuing state surveillance of religious instruction. The application of these criteria has generally served to discourage state aid to church-related elementary and secondary schools. Yet, the 1983 Supreme Court decision in *Mueller v. Allen* approved a Minnesota statute allowing a state income tax deduction for K-12 educational expenses, for both public and private school parents. However, a 1985 decision in a New York case, *Aguilar v. Felton,* restricted the flow of federally funded Chapter 1 monies to church-related schools.

Current interest in private school choice has led to speculation that states will soon come forth to challenge these decisions. In Arizona, a legal opinion prepared for the governor's office concludes: "There is no reason that a properly designed and administered school voucher system could not survive constitutional scrutiny. . . . In reality, this may be more of a political concern than a legal or constitutional concern" (Sheane & Bierlein, 1991, p. C-3). Using this information, a state task force recommended the inclusion of a private school choice system with both nonsectarian and sectarian schools as part of a major reform package.

Some speculate that the changing composition of the U.S. Supreme Court could serve to declare the inclusion of sectarian schools in a private school choice program as constitutional. John Coons notes, "There is no longer any serious doubt that it is valid to use public funds for education in religious schools if the subsidy is properly designed. . . . But, doubtless, this point will have to be litigated before the die-hard opposition will concede" (Negin, 1991, p. 11). Until that time, the separation of church and state continues to play a role in the choice debate.

Private School Supremacy

Many Americans believe that private schools offer a better education for those who can afford this alternative. This belief supports the perception that many public school students would consider transferring to a private school if the state supported their tuition. However, research in support of private school supremacy is mixed. For example, several researchers have revealed a small private-public gap (Chubb & Moe, 1990; Coleman, 1991). Others challenge the significance of these findings (Levin, 1991a; Witte, 1991a). Hence, a great debate has begun over whether private school students indeed outperform public school students.

Leading the charge is AFT President Albert Shanker. Using data from the 1990 National Assessment of Educational Progress (NAEP) mathematics assessment, Shanker notes that at the 12th-grade level, private school students performed only slightly better than those in public school. He points out that since most students in private schools are typically more economically advantaged, they should greatly outperform public school students. Witte (1991a) also attacks those who use these relatively small increases to propose a complete revamping of the public school system. He cites work by Alexander and Pallas that puts the magnitude of the Catholic school effect in substantive terms: "Differences are so trivial that if we could change public schools to look like Catholic schools on relevant factors, it would shift the public schools only from the 50th percentile ranking on standardized tests to the 53rd percentile" (p. 20). Levin (1991a) uses these same data to indicate that almost half of private school students have achievement scores below the average of public school students. He concludes that "private schools have a very slight advantage over public schools in terms of efficiency level. Whether this very nominal difference would be exacerbated with greater competition in a market choice system is a matter of speculation" (p. 276).

Other test data offered by Shanker and extracted from an article by Rothman (1991) illustrate a similar trend. Where differences occur, they are not significantly larger. For example:

- On the mathematics portion of the Scholastic Aptitude Test (SAT), public school students outscored those from private religious schools by one point (473 to 472) on a 200-to-800 scale. However, those from private independent schools scored an average of 542.
- On the 1990 American College Testing Program examination, public school students earned a composition score of 20.6 out of 35; those from private schools earned 21.0; and those from Catholic schools, 21.1.

Other researchers that support private choice point out that within these same data sets, large differences can be found. For example:

- The 1990 NAEP math assessment showed that at the 4th-grade level, the average proficiency for the public schools was 214; for Catholic schools, 224; and for private schools, 231. The gap at the 8th-grade level was 10 points.
- In NAEP's 1988 writing assessment, the average 4th-grade public school score was 189.4; for those in the nonpublic schools, 203.4. At the 8th-grade level, the average public school score was 206.7; in nonpublic schools, 231.3. At the 12th-grade level, in public schools it was 222.1; in nonpublic schools, 236.7.

In addition to offering data that highlight large differences, researchers who advocate private school superiority indicate that by 12th grade, many of the potentially low-scoring students have already dropped out of the public school, but similar students remain in the private school system. Therefore, public school scores would be even lower if their dropouts were still in school. They also argue that public high school scores benefit from an infusion of students who had attended private elementary schools.

Beyond test score issues, other choice advocates indicate that the school climate offered by many private schools is more conducive to learning, especially for urban minority populations, and that students tend to take more academic course work than their public school peers. Raywid (1989) states:

> Since public schools of choice, as well as private schools, are likely to have a distinctive, identifiable focus, they attract a group that is like-minded in some educationally significant way. To the extent that teachers, parents, and students agree on a mission, a commitment is generated that enables the school to become an effective learning community. (p. 14)

As has been shown, research data abounds to support both sides of the argument. There is no definitive answer to whether private schooling produces higher student achievement scores, but recent comparative data have certainly advanced the policy debate.

Bureaucratic Entrenchment

Advocates repeatedly indicate that those opposed to choice are primarily trying to protect their own turf. They offer examples of how strongly in favor the general public is, compared to those within the educational arena. They challenge that educational bureaucracies have been designed to protect the system, not the students (Doyle, 1989;

Finn, 1991; Kirkpatrick, 1990). Evidence is offered that teachers and parents are more positive within schools of choice, and that student achievement and attitudes improve (Nathan, 1989a). Even choice critics agree that "opposition to public school choice is not always free of self-interest" (Lieberman, 1990, p. 134).

Farrell (1990) offers an interesting example that supports these claims. As Representative Williams' private school choice bill was being debated, an alternative bill was posed by the Milwaukee Public Schools (MPS). Under this bill, MPS would have contracted with the private schools, rather than having parents seek enrollment directly, and the district would have been allowed to keep 10% of the voucher funding for administrative purposes. This caused a debate over who should determine the nature of a student's education, the parents or public school administrators.

To this end, choice advocates have not only endorsed the inclusion of private schools, but also addressed the need to break down the public school bureaucracy. Until recently, most choice plans have assumed that public schools would remain part of school districts. However, with the onslaught of decentralization debates, many theoretical models now envision that public schools would be able to "free" themselves of their districts and operate as a completely autonomous unit.

John Chubb and Terry Moe (1990) advocate such a proposal, based on the belief that school autonomy and freedom from bureaucratic constraints are critical factors in successful choice systems. Under their proposal, any public or private school meeting minimum state standards could receive direct state funding from regional "choice offices." Each student would be credited with a scholarship worth a differing amount, depending on certain student characteristics (e.g., handicapped students would receive a larger scholarship), and schools could not charge parents additional tuition. Current school districts and boards would continue to exist, but with jurisdiction over only those public schools wishing to remain governed. Individual schools would be allowed to establish their own nondiscriminatory admission criteria, but a safety net guaranteeing each student a school would be developed. Parent information centers also would be initiated, while teacher certification requirements would be minimal and tenure laws would be repealed.

Critics immediately began to attack Chubb and Moe's proposal on the lack of specifics and because creation of choice offices and parent information centers would ultimately create more, not less, state bureaucracy. Rather than 15,000-plus district central offices, additional administrative responsibility would be created at more than 83,000 public schools nationwide. Langley (1990) and Bastian (1989) also object to other hidden costs of administrating a choice system, such as additional transportation, the distribution of information to parents, and at least minimal oversight of private schools.

Under Chubb and Moe's proposal, a system of autonomous public schools would be created. Teachers would continue to have bargaining rights, but the legally prescribed bargaining unit would be the independent school. Lieberman (1990), however, finds this totally impractical and logistically unrealistic. For example, the New York City Board of Education negotiates at least 34 contracts with 10 different unions representing teachers, psychologists, school social workers, paraprofessionals, secretaries, custodians, medical personnel, and a host of other employee groups. In 1988 the New York City Board of Education operated 993 schools, and if each school were to have set its own personnel policies and administered its own budget, nearly 27,000 union contracts would have been negotiated. Lieberman states that administrative costs would be astronomical under any scenario treating individual schools as bargaining units. He indicates that choice advocates need to address the difficult issue of repealing state bargaining laws. If not, choice would not reduce the bureaucratic differential between public and private schools. Tenure and reduction in force (RIF) laws also need to be considered. Will choice increase efficiency, excellence, and equity? The dialogue continues.

Summary Snapshot of the Debate

As shown, the debate on choice is lengthy and complex. The general debate can be woven around the following arguments.

Advocates generally say:

- Choice is a way to achieve equal educational opportunity for poor and minority youngsters.
- Choice can rescue children from bad schools.
- Competition for students and money will force schools to improve and be more accountable.

- Children have different learning needs and, therefore, need different teaching options.
- By choosing a school, parents will be more involved in, and committed to, their child's education.
- Choice can promote voluntary desegregation.
- Choice will force schools/districts to streamline their bureaucracies.
- Choice will lead to a higher level of professionalism and expertise among teachers.

Critics generally say:

- There is no convincing evidence that competition will improve schools or pupil achievement.
- The children most in need—those without supportive, capable parents—will likely be left with the worst choices.
- Choice will work against low-income families unless transportation is provided; money spent on buses is better spent in the classroom.
- Private school choice will drain money from already needy public schools.
- Choice is a red herring that diverts the public's attention from the need to adequately finance public schools.
- Encouraging student transfers will undercut efforts to increase school-community ties.

The Future

What does the future hold for school choice? In Arizona, recommendations of Governor Fife Symington's Task Force on Educational Reform included choice as one of six major components. If passed by the legislature, choice would begin within public schools and, once a set of conditions were met, sectarian and nonsectarian private schools would be allowed to participate. These conditions include significant deregulation and decentralization of the public schools, as well as increased funding to cover the costs of special education, limited English proficient, and private school pupils. Private schools would be eligible to receive state funding equal to that of public schools, but would be required to meet all state and federal education laws. In essence, they would become public schools. Choice advocates are concerned that it will take years to accomplish the conditions, and even then, private schools may not want to participate because of the restrictions. Advocates want a "level playing field." These recommendations came as a result of 6 months of task force debates and 5 years of legislative activity to implement a public school choice system. As with most compromises, neither side is happy with the outcome, and the concept was soundly defeated by the legislature during spring 1992.

In California, 1992 also looked to be a busy year for potential choice activities. Assembly Bill 614 sought to establish a public school choice program. More controversial, however, was an attempt by the Excellence through Choice in Education League (EXCEL), to place a private school voucher initiative on the fall 1992 ballot. The constitutional amendment would have provided annual vouchers worth approximately $2,500 toward private school tuition. Estimates placed the cost at more than $2 billion. Advocates, including some business and church leaders, claimed the measure would spur competition and result in a higher quality of education. Opponents, including state school superintendent Bill Honig and the California Teachers Association, called it a tax break for the rich that could bankrupt the state's public school system (Amsler, 1992). Although adequate signatures were not verified in time for the fall 1992 ballot, the initiative will be placed before voters during fall 1994.

During December 1991 the Pennsylvania legislature defeated a choice bill that would have given parents a $900 voucher to spend on private school tuition. During February 1992 the Florida legislature rejected a school choice voucher that would have included private schools. The sponsor of the defeated bill said it was no longer a matter of *if* his bill will pass, but *when.* Also during February 1992 Maryland's Governor William Schaefer offered support for a 5-year pilot program that would allow 100 students from schools with the lowest achievement scores to attend any public, private, or parochial school in the state (American Political Network, Inc., 1992a, 1992d). Finally, Colorado voters will decide in November 1992 whether to implement a voucher system that would include private sectarian and nonsectarian schools as well as home schoolers.

These are just a few of many battles recently fought across the country. The general feeling is that many states will be implementing public school choice provisions as a means to hold off the private school forces. Kearns and Doyle (1988) repeatedly warned the public schools that private school choice is virtually assured unless radical change occurs:

Schools have much to gain if they heed the lesson, everything to lose if they do not. The schools are not yet forced to compete, but if they continue to fail their charges, if reform does not catch hold, schools will be subject to a spontaneous market test. Bright flight will continue. The old patrons of the public schools will finally abandon them for private alternatives, or for public schools that will respond. And the public schools that ignore business' most important lesson—that markets and competition work— will wake up one morning with no one to teach and nothing to do. (p. 127)

Several professional educational organizations have felt compelled to change their anti-choice stance. The National Association of Secondary School Principals (NASSP) has "cautiously endorsed" school choice among public and private schools. The 43,000-member organization now supports choice as long as all schools are required to follow the same mandates regarding the selection, admission, and retention of all students. The policy also states, however, that choice in and of itself will not improve education to the degree necessary to achieve the National Education Goals (American Political Network, Inc., 1992b).

The American Federation of Teachers has also reversed its position. In a recent advertisement, AFT President Albert Shanker commented, "Our schools are in bad shape. Changes, big changes are needed. Public school choice, by itself, is not the big change that we need, but it may be that we can't get the big changes we need without choice" (Lieberman, 1990, p. 111). The National Education Association (NEA) also now supports public school choice, but only under specific conditions. Neither organization supports private school involvement.

A Clash of Basic Values and Freedoms

The choice debate can be summed up rather easily. It involves a debate about the freedom to choose a school for one's child. However, several basic freedoms form a democratic system—freedom of conscience, freedom of thought, freedom of choice—and if any one freedom is unrestricted, it conflicts with others. Therefore, the maintenance of a system of liberties involves balancing each freedom against the others.

Frances Fowler (1991) reviews how school choice serves to balance or unbalance these freedoms by analyzing France's educational system.

Since 1959, the "Debré Act" has provided public funding for private schools under a set of conditions, whereby the greater the financial subsidy chosen by the private school, the more government control. Those accepting full subsidies must follow government regulations covering teacher credentials, curriculum, hours of instruction offered weekly; submit to financial audits; and accept children of all religions and backgrounds. They have the right to maintain a distinctive character, but must respect their pupils' freedom of conscience.

Fowler indicates that the debate in France more than 30 years ago was quite similar to the current one in America. Choice advocates voiced the danger of a government monopoly over education, saying that genuine democracy depends on granting citizens the right to choose a school. They believed that public resources must be devoted to maintaining institutions necessary for political liberty and that refusal to subsidize private schools was a violation of the democratic principles of freedom of conscience and equality.

Choice critics were no less vocal. They believed that the importance of children's freedom of thought far outweighed the freedom of parents, religious leaders, and other parties involved in education. They were concerned that private schools (especially private religious schools) taught the academic disciplines from a particular perspective and restricted the intellectual stimulation resulting from exposure to people from different backgrounds.

The resulting law was designed to balance these freedoms. Private schools could maintain their distinctive character, but they must teach with complete respect for children's freedom of conscience. As a result, private schools have become more schools of the nation than schools of the church. Fowler concludes that the French successfully balanced the freedom of private groups to establish schools, the freedom of parents to choose private schools, and the students' freedom of thought and conscience. However, this was only because the law incorporated both sides of the issue—it was viewed not as a compromise, but as a careful balance of liberty.

In the United States, there is little attempt to balance these freedoms since both sides believe compromise means a complete loss. Choice advocates focus primarily on parents as consumers and schools as products, rather than concentrating on basic freedoms as the French had. On the other hand, American critics refuse to accept parental freedom as being equally important. Agreement can be reached, but it depends upon a complex understanding of what freedom means in a democratic society. Until some element of balance similar to the French system can be achieved, choice will remain a major controversial public policy issue for decades to come. As John Witte (1991b) concludes:

> Proponents of choice stress the primary value of liberty, a more equitable dispersion of that liberty, and pluralistic diversity. Opponents of choice stress equality, an integrated society, and common school traditions. Philosophers have been debating these value differences for thousands of years. It is no wonder that these arguments divide well-intentioned parents, education providers, and policy experts. (p. 9)

6

Can Schools Do It All?

Introduction

The current American education system was built upon the belief that all people are created equal and thus should have equality of educational opportunity. Thanks to Horace Mann and his fellow reformers, the common school was believed to have the capacity to provide young Americans with the independence needed to resist selfishness and vindictiveness. It was thought that education enabled individuals to pursue success, and therefore equipped them to be good citizens and lead lives of freedom and productiveness. It comes as no surprise that from the very beginning of mass education in the United States, schooling was believed to be the common denominator. Schools, in conjunction with home, community, and church, were to have large responsibilities in carrying out American ideals.

Former Secretary of Education William Bennett writes in his recent book, *Devaluing of America: The Fight for Our Culture and Our Children* (1992):

> There are values that all American citizens share and that we should want all American students to know and to make their own: honesty, fairness, self-discipline, fidelity to task, friends, and family, personal responsibility, love of country, and belief in the principles of liberty, equality and

the freedom to practice one's faith. The explicit teaching of these values is the legacy of the common school, and it is a legacy to which we must return. . . . Students should finish high school knowing not just the "method" or "process" of science or history; they should actually know some science and history. They should know fractions and decimals, and percentages and algebra and geometry. They should know that for every action there is an equal and opposite reaction, and they should know who said "I am the state" and who said "I have a dream." They should know about subjects and predicates, about isosceles triangles and ellipses. They should know where the Amazon flows, and what the First Amendment means. They should know about the Donner party and slavery, and Shylock, Hercules, and Abigail Adams, where Ethiopia is, and why there was a Berlin Wall. They should know how a poem works, how a plant works, and the meaning of "If wishes were horses, beggars would ride." (pp. 58, 61)

In addition to the large task of supporting students' academic and moral well-being as noted above, several societal roles for schooling also exist. Henry Levin (1991b) states that in a democratic and capitalist society, education has several major roles that bear on economic well-being. Schools must provide youths with skills, attitudes, values, and behaviors essential for economic productivity. This investment in human capital will increase the future economic productivity not only of the students but also of society as a whole. Schools must also redress inequality, especially among persons born into different social circumstances, so that differences in the social origins of children are not reproduced in adulthood.

But can schools do it all? Over time, people have turned to schools to solve or at least mitigate society's concerns. Since the early days of mass immigration, schools have been called upon to instill democratic values into America's newcomers. The War on Poverty during the 1960s was fought in the classrooms through Chapter 1 compensatory programs; bilingual programming was advanced to support the ever-growing limited English proficient population. During the 1970s schools were asked to make up for the injustices of segregation through forced busing. The 1980s continued to bring attention to the need to eliminate gender biases, while the 1990s bring distribution of condoms as schools tackle the AIDS battle. Most agree that these activities, and dozens more like them, are essential humane tasks. However, many contend academics have been neglected because of these additional responsibilities. Educators note that in the absence of adequate social service support for families, schools are left to face these issues. If a child is hungry, or must stay home to take care of siblings, then little learning can occur.

To give the reader a sense of the many societal concerns schools are asked to address, this chapter will review a sample of the issues—bilingual education, desegregation and busing, and support for disadvantaged youth.

The Bilingual Education Debate

The evolution of bilingual education portrays a good example of how social needs and political forces shape our country's educational public policies. Although not at the top of the current controversial issues list, bilingual education policy debates echoed through the halls of Congress and state legislatures during the 1970s and 1980s; the furor of state "English Only" initiatives has only recently subsided. Although the cries of racism that permeated these debates are no longer in the headlines, actions taken over the past 2 decades continue to dictate how limited English proficient students are to be educated in our public schools. This section will briefly discuss the history of this debate, key political forces, primary outcomes, and its current status.

First, working definitions for several terms are important. *Bilingual education* involves the use of the child's native language to teach content and skills, with a transfer of this knowledge into the second language (English) once the initial skills have been mastered. The ultimate goal is to enable the limited English proficient (LEP) pupil to achieve competency and literacy in both languages. Focus is also given to teaching the history and culture of the United States, as well as customs and values of the cultures associated with the languages being taught. *English as a Second Language* (ESL) programs provide instruction in English language development as well as other core subject areas, using instructional practices that have been modified to make the material more comprehensible to LEP students. In some cases, the child's native language is utilized only to the degree that it is necessary for the child to understand the concept in English; however, in many cases, the teacher is a monolingual English-speaker, and therefore the child's native language is not utilized at all. The overall goal is to have the student become fluent in English as soon as possible. *Language immersion* programs follow models successfully utilized in Canada, whereby instruction is provided in English, yet the instructor employs the student's native language to provide additional assistance/clarification as needed. In reality, a combination of these instructional strategies is utilized by various districts, depending upon philosophical beliefs and on the availability of teachers fluent in multiple languages. The practice of *language submersion* or "sink or swim" has been utilized in the past and occasionally today. However, court rulings have found that submersion, or the absence of specific services for LEP students, violates protections granted to such students under the Civil Rights Act of 1964 and the Equal Educational Opportunities Act of 1974.

Embedded within debates over the effectiveness of these various strategies are two extreme viewpoints. Some, who are frequently ultraconservatives, view LEP students as handicapped and in need of remedial assistance due to a language deficiency; see America as a monolingual, English-speaking society; and see assimilation as the best way for LEP students to enter the mainstream of school and society quickly. Others, commonly liberals, view the student's primary language as an untapped resource for the student and for the country; see America as a multilingual society with English as a national language common to all; and support the goal of English development, but include other primary languages in the curriculum as a means of cultural enrichment for all children (Barry, 1983). These dialectical views serve to divide people into two general categories, "cultural uniformists" or "cultural pluralists," although many fall somewhere in between.

While policymakers argue on theoretical grounds, schools have had to address the real issue of educating language-minority children in the classroom. During 1989-1990, there were approximately 2 million LEP school-age children, which represented more than 5% of all students (U.S. Department of Education, 1991). In New Mexico, this encompassed more than 18% of their student population, while in California it was more than 16%. The number of language-minority children continues to grow steadily, placing tremendous responsibility on schools with limited resources. In addition, research results are conflicting, thus allowing the political mood of the country and each community to dictate teaching methodology. Many educators have become frustrated with the mixed messages received regarding goals for educating LEP children. A former teacher and the author of *Forked Tongue: Politics of Bilingual Education,* Rosalie Pedalino Porter (1990), expressed her frustration with the rigidity of a bilingual education program used by her district:

When I gave the required thirty minutes of English-language lessons in the kindergarten, scrupulously separate from the Spanish teaching and of much shorter duration, the students responded with equal enthusiasm. . . . I do not know how they felt about the patchwork use of two languages in the classroom, but I know how I felt: odd at first, and then very doubtful about the efficacy of what I was doing. (p. 21)

Just as Pedalino Porter expressed doubt at the merits of bilingual education, others report its success and value for all children. A brief history follows to highlight our country's struggle with this issue.

The United States' Early Use of Bilingual Education

The melting pot is an image most Americans are quite familiar with: America is a nation of immigrants, people who came here for a better life, glad to abandon their native language and culture for those of their new country. Transformed by their experiences, they emerged as Americans. This romanticized version of reality says very little about how this supposed melting occurred, or even whether immigrants found it desirable. History indicates that it did not take place easily. The immigrants' children were typically the first to achieve fluency in English, their grandchildren the first to finish high school, and their great-grandchildren the first to grow up in the middle class. The immigrants survived, but not without much struggle and hardship. They came to America for a multitude of reasons, but not to escape their heritage. In fact, most groups fought to preserve their cultures while in America. While they saw a need to learn the language of their new country, they also wanted to keep their own heritage alive.

Bilingual education has existed in the United States since the late 1600s, when German-speaking Americans opened schools providing instruction in both German and English (U.S. Department of Education, 1991). In general, our forefathers accepted bilingualism as a fact of life. The Continental Congress published many official documents in German and French, and evidence suggests that the framers of the U.S. Constitution believed that a democracy should leave language choices to the individual. By the mid-1800s, state laws had authorized the instruction of children in languages other than English (e.g., German was allowed in Ohio; French in Louisiana). By 1900 more than 600,000 American children (about 4% of the elementary school population at the time) were receiving instruction partly or exclusively in German.

Although some instances of language repression occurred in America's history (many due to the anti-Catholic fervor during the late 1880s, and new waves of Italian, Jewish, and Slavic immigrants during the early 1900s), tolerance of language differences was the norm until the onset of World War I. Then, a wave of nationalism occurred, whereby proficiency in English was increasingly equated with political loyalty. State laws were passed banning German speech in the classroom as well as in the street. The notion of Anglo-conformity resulted in hostility toward all minority languages, and 15 states legislated English as the basic language of instruction. Soon after Nebraska's law was struck down by the U.S. Supreme Court in 1923 as being too restrictive, the fervor of Americanization began to subside. Public attitudes, however, had changed fundamentally; learning in languages other than English seemed less than patriotic.

In the years following World War II, LEP children came to be viewed as "culturally disadvantaged" or "educationally handicapped." Psychologists considered inadequate English language skills as an environmental factor explaining poor school performance. English as a Second Language (ESL) courses were prescribed for these students. However, as noted in a Civil Rights Commission survey at that time, "most ESL classes fail to expose children to approaches, attitudes, and materials which take advantage of the rich Mexican American heritage. . . . When children are painfully ashamed of who they are, they are not going to do very well in school" (Crawford, 1989, p. 26).

A rebirth of bilingual education came during the early 1960s as the first Cuban immigrants arrived in Miami. Using the talents of these immigrants, the Miami schools began to provide full-fledged bilingual programs for English and Spanish speakers with a goal of fluent bilingualism for both groups. The programs met with great success and gained visibility. At the same time, national attention was directed at the high dropout rates among language-minority children because the economy could no longer rely upon uneducated and unskilled labor. The civil rights movement was also energizing language-minority parents. These growing pressures served to initiate federal policies that supported bilingual education as a means to provide equity for all students.

As an outcome of the Civil Rights Act of 1964, a series of court decisions occurred on whether placing language-minority students in "sink or swim" classrooms violated students' rights to equal educational opportunities. The U.S. Supreme Court's *Lau v. Nichols* decision found that students' rights were breached, and required schools to provide additional support to LEP students. In response, the Office for Civil Rights (OCR) developed very specific guidelines referred to as the Lau Remedies and began to review school districts with large numbers of minority children to ensure compliance. These guidelines required districts to provide bilingual education for LEP elementary students; ESL programs were acceptable only at the high school level. As a result, hundreds of bilingual programs were set up under the OCR's Lau Remedies.

Also during this time, Congress passed the Bilingual Education Act of 1968 (i.e., Title VII of the Elementary and Secondary Education Act), providing limited federal funding for bilingual education programs. Initially, the programs were to focus on LEP students who also met poverty criteria, since overall funding was limited. Later, the 1973-1974 reauthorization dropped the poverty criterion and expanded program funding. However, it was unclear whether the goal of the act was to increase the rate of English language acquisition by students with limited English skills, or to promote bilingualism in all students. This central question was an indication of the pending controversy over bilingual education.

The Return of the Melting Pot

A number of factors conspired to swing the pendulum back toward ESL programs after a period of relative acceptance of bilingual education. A growing number of cultural conformists believed that pluralism was (and is) a matter of local choice and not a proper responsibility of the federal government. They advocated that the goal of Title VII should be to assist children of limited- or non-English-speaking ability to gain competency in English as quickly as possible so that they may enjoy equal educational opportunities.

Debate also increased when the American Institute for Research released its major evaluation of bilingual education in 1978. The study found no evidence that children in bilingual education programs were better off than those not receiving additional help. The study concluded that most bilingual education programs were primarily used for minority language maintenance rather than a transition to English; Spanish-speaking children were retained in bilingual education programs even after their English skills were sufficient for them to be in a regular classroom. Although the study was criticized for drawing conclusions from evaluations of widely disparate programs, it fueled the debate.

Shortly thereafter, several other key studies surfaced, disputing the effectiveness of bilingual education programs. For example, the 1981 Baker-de Kanter report concluded that evidence supporting the effectiveness of bilingual education was tenuous at best, although Ann Willig's 1985 meta-analysis of the same data showed significant positive results.

At the same time, the OCR's implementation of the Lau Remedies was becoming controversial due to their restrictiveness; indeed, funding to several school districts was cut because the OCR deemed their treatment of LEP students insufficient. District resistance, coupled with conflicting research and the Reagan administration's push for a new federalism, caused Congress to modify the Bilingual Education Act in 1984. They determined that within federally funded programs, minority languages could be used only to help a child achieve competence in the English language, and that funding could not be given to language maintenance programs. In response to growing pressure, Secretary of Education Terrell Bell withdrew the Lau Remedies, and monitoring of programs by OCR decreased significantly. The tide had turned quickly against bilingual education.

Following years of heavy government involvement in district-level LEP programs, the Reagan administration's hands-off attitude was welcomed by many who felt that development of programs should be left to the expertise of local districts. Continued attempts were made to change the federal laws, from removing the native-language requirement for Title VII grants to proposal of a constitutional amendment to make English the official language of the United States. Although anti-bilingual sentiments continued to grow, liberal forces in Congress were able to minimize more radical federal changes.

No longer having the support of OCR and the U.S. Department of Education, bilingual education advocates turned instead to the Equal Educational Opportunities Act (EEOA) of 1974 as a defense. In *Castaneda v. Pickard,* the U.S. Fifth Circuit Court of Appeals interpreted the EEOA to require language assistance programs for LEP students. The court stated that such programs must meet three criteria: (a) based on a sound educational theory; (b) implemented effectively, with adequate resources and personnel; and (c) evaluated as effective in overcoming language handicaps after a trial period (Lyons, 1989). Under these provisions, many bilingual programs continued, but predominately within local communities that offered strong support for cultural plurality.

Other districts bowed to both internal and external pressures and offered primarily ESL instruction.

The "English Only" Movement

Taking advantage of changing attitudes, the powerful and well-organized "U.S. English" group (frequently referred to as English Only) came into power. Organized as an offshoot of the Federation for American Immigration Reform (FAIR), U.S. English delivered a simple message: Because the English language has been the bond holding our society together, our common language is threatened when there is a mindless drift toward a bilingual society. The climate was right for official English efforts. As Crawford (1989) explains:

> Language politics, formerly a minor theme in American history, has taken on a new urgency in the 1980s. U.S. English has crystallized a growing unease with bilingualism, or more precisely, with the perceived indifference toward English among recent immigrants. To many, these newcomers seem content to live in insular communities where they can work, shop, go to school, worship, watch television, and even vote in their native languages. Hispanics and Asians are transforming some cities to the extent that some English speakers feel like strangers in their own neighborhoods. Perhaps most galling to monolingual Americans, government is promoting programs like bilingual education that appear to encourage cultural Balkanization. (p. 54)

The English Only viewpoint became very popular, as evidenced by a membership of 350,000 and an annual budget of $7 million in 1988. It found a receptive ear among Americans of diverse backgrounds and political persuasions. Many believed that bilingual education was actually holding people back, and that an official-English amendment would help immigrants master the language. Others firmly believed that well-developed bilingual education programs were in the best interest of not only the individual student but also our pluralist society. Nonetheless, as of 1988, U.S. English had spent more than $18 million within 39 state campaigns to pass "official English" legislation. Momentum grew to the point where a federal constitutional amendment to make English the official language of the country was once again being considered. U.S. English was also involved in state campaigns to limit the use of foreign languages, as evidenced by its effort to eliminate the Spanish Yellow

Pages, Spanish-language advertising by public utilities, and phone bills printed in Chinese.

However, a series of events soon began to unravel the power of the English Only movement. Within the organization, memos linking the group to immigration restriction groups, population control organizations, and a eugenics organization led to the resignation of its president, Linda Chavez, and the abandonment of endorsements by such public figures as Walter Cronkite (Crawford, 1988). By the early 1990s little was heard about the work of U.S. English. However, the adoption of English Only initiatives in many states, and a 3-year limitation on students' placement in federally supported bilingual programs, are examples of the policy changes that were made during the mid-1980s at the height of the organization's power.

Bilingual Education in the 1990s

As shown, this issue has been a tug-of-war between liberal and conservative views. Initially, bilingual education was the norm during the early history of our country and remained that way until World War I generated anti-German sentiments. A drive for nationalism during the 1930s returned most LEP students to ESL classes, or they were left to sink or swim, with little regard for maintenance of other cultures. Successful experiments with bilingual education programs and a series of court cases during the civil rights era helped swing the pendulum back toward bilingualism. During the 1980s a new federalism ideal and the English Only movement quickly pulled policies back toward the goal of advancing English as quickly as possible. Throughout the decades, policymakers have followed the political mood of the country and have often heeded the warnings of cultural uniformists. The lack of quality research and outcomes only served to muddle the debate.

Now, in the 1990s, international competition and a world economy are causing many to rethink America's predominantly monolingual stance. For example, in 1992 the Arizona State Board of Education mandated that all students master certain foreign language competencies by the end of third and eighth grades. Other states have similar initiatives. A 1991 longitudinal study completed by the U.S. Department of Education, showing that bilingual education effectively educates LEP students, may finally settle the research debate (Ramirez, Yuen, & Ramey, 1991). However, as with other research reports on this topic, critics content that the study was flawed. The debate is far from over, especially at the local district level, where educators are faced with a growing population of LEP students, declining revenues, conflicting research results, and a segment of our society that is threatened by the ever-growing diversity among our country's citizens. Educators are caught between a desire to do what is best for language-minority students and a society that has not yet come to terms with how best to inculcate American values.

Desegregation and Busing

This section discusses another issue in which schools have been asked to play a key role—the debate over school desegregation. Since the late 1950s emotions have run high over the impact that mandated, court-ordered desegregation (e.g., busing) has had on the lives, safety, and happiness of children and families ordered to comply with busing. It is perhaps the one issue that best illuminates the great differences between our nation's ideals of equity and the resistance by society to the realities of implementing these ideals.

Historical Antecedents of Busing

To fully understand the significance of busing and the issues surrounding its implementation, one first needs to examine the landmark civil rights decisions that led to busing. In 1869 the Supreme Court ruled in *Plessy v. Ferguson* that the practice of "separate but equal" was constitutional. As a result, separate schools, parks, waiting rooms, hotels, restrooms, and drinking fountains were allocated to each race; however, few could claim their equality. Where it was not possible to provide separate facilities, each race was given its own particular part of any given facility.

In May 1954 the Supreme Court overturned the Plessy doctrine with *Brown v. Board of Education of Topeka,* pronouncing that separate educational facilities are inherently unequal and that segregating children on the basis of race deprives minority children of equal education opportunities. The court focused on the original intent of the Fourteenth Amendment, which states that no state shall make or enforce any law which shall abridge the privileges or immunities of citizens of the United States, and all citizens have a right to due process and equal protection. One key issue in the decision was the psychologically devastating effect of segregation on black children and the resulting inequities. Through *Brown,* it was determined that equal protection applied to everyone, including minorities.

Public education represented the opportunity to reshape young minds, both intellectually and attitudinally, and therefore was to become a vital part of this debate. School integration, however, was not to be achieved easily. Technically, the only parties bound by the Supreme Court decision were the five school boards involved in the suit. Thus, it required individual lawsuits to be filed in each county or major city before courts compelled school districts to initiate school desegregation activities (Cushman, 1976). Southern states, where the greatest concern over segregation was centered, developed elaborate procedures and legislation to resist school integration; between 1954 and 1958, 11 southern states enacted 145 statutes to exempt themselves from the court rulings. Many white school administrators argued that the best approach was to acclimate whites to the idea of integration slowly (e.g., grade-a-year phase-in programs). Violence was also a concern, as shown by the dynamiting of a school in Nashville because it allowed 13 black children to register in an all-white school. As incidents of racially motivated violence occurred, whites became polarized, either joining efforts to combat the injustices facing black children attending school or picketing against the idea of schools being opened to blacks. Ten years after the passage of *Brown,* only 12% of public schools in the 11-state southern region were desegregated; in the deep South (Georgia, Alabama, and Mississippi) just 2% of the schools were integrated.

The passage of the Civil Rights Act in 1964 gave the government a new way to control desegregation. Title VI of the act was used to cut off federal funding to school districts for failing to comply with the 1954 *Brown* decision. In addition, the attorney general could use Title VI to file suits against public schools for not desegregating (Edelman, 1973). The Department of Health, Education and Welfare (HEW) also became a major administrative enforcer with its power to withhold funds from noncomplying schools. During the 10 years following the passage of the Civil Rights Act, the Justice Department initiated 500 school desegregation suits, and HEW brought 600 more actions.

Cultural Conflict: The Busing Debate and "White Flight"

Because segregation was so deeply rooted in society and thus within the schools, mandated busing and strong court oversight were initiated as remedies for school segregation. Busing has always been viewed as a means to an end—equalized educational opportunity among races. Proponents of busing have not been for busing so much as they have been for what it would accomplish. They believed improvements in academic achievement and self-esteem of blacks, along with the teaching of new social values to all children, could be achieved in integrated schools. Since districts initially refused to deal with the issue voluntarily, the courts viewed mandated busing as the only solution. In 1971 the Supreme Court upheld the authority of lower courts to require busing of students between all-black and all-white schools in *Swann v. Charlotte-Mecklenburg Board of Education.* In later cases the Court also set guidelines specifying the extent to which lower courts could regulate school boards' desegregation plans.

During the implementation of such busing plans, the phenomenon of "white flight" became a dominant research topic for social scientists. The question was whether desegregation plans would cause a percentage of white families to either move to a county that did not have busing or enroll their children in private schools. Research results were inconsistent, depending upon the methodology employed; some researchers found no white flight while others saw whites leaving in droves. Although private school enrollment generally declined between 1959 and 1975, many cities where busing was implemented saw private school enrollment increase sharply. Yet this finding was contested by other researchers, who said that other cities without court-ordered busing experienced similar increases.

By the late 1970s, however, there was general agreement that white flight did exist. Studies examining causes found no evidence that discipline problems, lower achievement scores or grades, differences in texts, curricula, or the quality of teachers were the reasons for whites leaving public schools. Instead, many researchers believed it was deep-rooted cultural bias, as shown by the following:

> To many whites, the black culture represented values they abhorred. The white middle-class values of self-discipline, hard work, real achievement, proper manners, and deserved merit were sacred. The black culture, as whites conceived of it, valued other things; otherwise, whites asked, why would there be so much violence, so many illegitimate children, and so many people on welfare in North Nashville? Busing could assimilate blacks to white cultural values, or it could assimilate whites to black cultural values. Many white parents, it seems, did not want to risk the latter. (Pride & Woodard, 1985, p. 142)

Others did not oppose black children being brought to their schools as much as their own white children being bused to formerly all-black "ghetto schools," viewed as inferior. In addition, many wanted to maintain the neighborhood school concept. For example, a 1977 survey of parents within the Los Angeles School District showed that although 86% of whites were opposed to busing of children of any racial background, 72% of whites had no objection to having large percentages of minorities bused to their school. The problem focused on two-way busing. Fifty-four percent of whites wanted their children to attend neighborhood schools, while 60% of Hispanics and 47% of blacks expressed similar beliefs (Armor, 1980).

On the other hand, research has consistently shown that integration does improve black children's academic performance, but it does not lower that of white children. An expansive review of the literature on busing and achievement determined that the ratio of studies finding positive effects of busing on achievement to those citing negative effects was four to one (Pride & Woodard, 1985). However, the issue of educational quality was of major concern for white parents, who felt their children's education was being compromised. It was of equal concern for black parents, who saw the gap in educational performance between black and white students not being narrowed sufficiently.

Busing in the North and the Rise of Magnet Alternatives

During the early 1970s focus turned toward desegregation issues in the North and West where, unlike the South, little progress was being made. However, in these areas, desegregation was a different task due to techniques applied to ensure segregation in the first place. These included gerrymandering district boundaries, which neatly split white and black neighborhoods, and district policies that allowed white families in racially mixed neighborhoods to transfer to all-white schools. Trying to terminate these tactics was difficult and did little to increase overall desegregation. As in the South, numerous court cases were filed, using *Swann v. Charlotte-Mecklenburg* as a foundation. During the early 1970s cities such as San Francisco, Denver, and Minneapolis were affected by such cases (Cushman, 1976).

However, alternatives to busing that lessened cultural conflicts were sought. As part of Minneapolis's plan to remedy segregation, the school board was allowed to continue its long-established magnet school program as an alternative to busing (e.g., fundamental schools; open schools). Enrollment in these schools was voluntary, and a racially mixed student body was the result. A new trend had begun. Cities that developed magnet programs under court order in the mid-1970s included Denver, Boston, Los Angeles, Dallas, Louisville, Milwaukee, and San Diego. Others, such as Chicago, Cincinnati, and Seattle, developed programs to offset the threat of a court order, while some cities developed completely voluntary magnet programs. However, not all have been able to utilize magnet schools as an alternative to busing. For example, the Wilmington, Delaware, magnet school proposal was denied by the court because there were no racial enrollment quotas and no guarantees that the programs would greatly reduce segregation in that area.

Current Desegregation Activities

The debate surrounding mandatory desegregation activities continues. A 1992 study by Gary Orfield reviews desegregation over the past 20 years and sheds new light on the plight of minorities in public education (National School Boards Association, 1992). Orfield suggests that some of the nation's suburbs and cities show patterns of resegregation. This is especially true where county-wide desegregation plans are not in place, thus allowing white flight to the suburbs. Segregation has increased during the late 1980s for black students in the Northeast and Midwest, while Hispanic students have experienced greater segregation in the West and Midwest. However, desegregation of Southern blacks actually increased from 1980 to 1988.

Anti-busing leaders are making strides to eliminate this activity in some cities. The Denver school board recently filed a motion with the U.S. District Court to end court-ordered busing. Its claim, as other cities have argued, is that the dual (separate but equal) school system that once caused court-ordered busing has been eliminated. Indeed, a landmark March 1992 Supreme Court decision, *Freeman v. Pitts,* has paved the way for less control by federal courts over desegregation plans. The court ruled that as long as government-endorsed racial segregation has ended, school districts are under no duty to remedy an imbalance caused by demographic factors. This means that it is not necessarily unconstitutional to have mostly black and mostly white schools in the same district if the same racial patterns occur in neighborhoods. Viewed as a setback for civil-rights groups, some believe that the decision is the first step in abandonment of the *Brown* decision.

This brief sketch of desegregation issues in the United States high-lights a struggle between equity and liberty, among other conflicts. In attempting to uphold the Fourteenth Amendment rights for all citizens, mandated busing has minimized freedom of choice for those involved. Many contend that the vast energy and resources expended on these matters have hindered efforts toward excellence. The recent *Freeman v. Pitts* Supreme Court ruling has swung the pendulum away from strong federal oversight back toward local district control. Overall, it shows how education has been used as a primary means to overcome a major social injustice and once again has been caught in the equity versus local control conflict. As shown by these recent activities, desegregation and busing issues have not been laid to rest. This is an indication of how difficult the matter is and the continued lack of consensus on what our societal goals should be, let alone how to achieve them.

Disadvantaged Youth

Few disagree that social conditions in this country have deteriorated in the recent past; no one knows this better than school personnel working with children on a daily basis. A quick review of several alarming statistics extracted from work by Harold Hodgkinson (1991) will illustrate key concerns:

- Since 1987 one-fourth of all preschool children in the United States have been in poverty.
- Every year about 350,000 children are born to mothers who were addicted to cocaine during pregnancy.
- Nearly 15 million children are being reared by single mothers whose income averages about $11,400 in 1988 dollars (within $1,000 of the poverty line).
- Twenty percent of America's preschool children have not been vaccinated against polio.
- The "Norman Rockwell" family—a working father, a housewife mother, and two children of school age—constitutes only 6% of U.S. households today.
- One-fourth of pregnant mothers receive no physical care of any sort during the crucial first trimester of pregnancy; about 20% of handicapped children would not be impaired had their mothers received even minimal prenatal care.
- On any given night, between 50,000 and 200,000 children have no home.

- In 1987 child protective agencies received 2.2 million reports of child abuse or neglect—triple the number received in 1976.

Impact on Schooling

Adequate discussion of the ramifications of these conditions on the welfare of American's children is beyond the scope of this book, but they are notable. Their impact on the role of schooling is also significant. Levin (1991b) writes:

> Any attempt to provide fairness in access to material rewards in a democratic and capitalist society must consider the initial unfairness experienced by children born into families characterized by poverty and other unenviable situations. Students from lower socioeconomic origins have poorer educational opportunities in their homes, as well as inferior medical care, nutrition, and shelter, than those from more advantaged origins. John Dewey once wrote that "It is the aim of progressive education to take part in correcting unfair privilege and unfair deprivation, not to perpetuate them." Therefore, it would be necessary for the educational system to intervene in the social system so that there is no systematic relation between a person's social origins or gender and his or her ultimate social attainments. (p. 130)

However, schools have limited time to take on these responsibilities. If students diligently attend class 6 hours a day, 180 days a year, from kindergarten through 12th grade, they will have spent just 9% of their lives in school. When family, church, and community groups (e.g., Little League, Scouts) were part of child development, the 9% schooling time was somewhat sufficient; however, social conditions have changed, and such supports are available to only a few. Even critics of the current public education structure acknowledge:

> When a six-year-old arrives in first grade without a basic vocabulary, lacking self-control, unaccustomed to books, hypnotized by television, and ignorant of the rudiments of group behavior, the school's leverage seems puny indeed. When a teenager lands in high school with a drug or alcohol habit, a baby of her own, a record of lawless behavior, a part-time job that runs well into the evening, or a gang membership that fills the wee hours with fighting and frivolity, it's not likely that a lot of book reports are going to get written or French verbs conjugated. (Finn, 1991, p. 22)

So what happens instead? Many of these students do not survive in the system; nearly 30% of America's students drop out of school. In many cases, this number would be much higher were it not for creative educators, dedicated community members, and concerned policymakers. Although the federal government has provided compensatory programs and Head Start funding since the 1960s, not until the 1980s did the states begin a major expansion of these programs through state-supported preschools and K-12 at-risk funding. In response, alternative schools for dropouts and potential dropouts exist across the country and are growing in number. Young mothers and fathers are coming to school with infants in their arms, learning both science and child development. Many additional children are receiving preschool and other educational services, while many schools are offering adult education classes for parents.

In addition, schools are becoming the hub of community services by running "one-stop" health or social service centers, or at least by serving as brokers for families into the social service system. For example, a district in New York City recently opened a comprehensive school/community center that is open year-round, 15 hours per day, 6 days a week, and offers medical and dental services; tutoring; drug counseling; workshops on pregnancy prevention, AIDS, and racial awareness; parenting classes; and other programs. Approximately 800 schools nationwide operate similar programs, with some states such as Florida requiring school-based health care for teen parents (American Political Network, Inc., 1992f). New York City schools are also distributing free condoms, while in Falmouth, Massachusetts, condom vending machines have been installed in the high school. Similar activities have also been implemented in Los Angeles, Philadelphia, Chicago, and San Francisco (Flax, 1991). Nearly all districts offer an AIDS education program, and many others are also considering condom distribution.

In Phoenix, the Arizona Department of Economic Security recently opened a satellite office on the grounds of an inner-city elementary school district. This office assists families with subsidies for day-care and food stamps, and distributes emergency assistance funds to those facing short-term crises. Staff also run a food bank and clothing closet, offer ESL and adult education classes, and provide job training and day-care (Donofrio, 1991). Kentucky's 1990 educational reform statutes prescribe family or youth resource centers either at or near every school where at least 20% of the students meet federal free lunch income criteria. To date, nearly $10 million has been appropriated for these centers in Kentucky, with projected costs reaching nearly $30 million by 1993-1994 (Jalomo & Bierlein, 1991b). Finally, as an example of how extensive a role schools could play, U.S. Senator John McCain of Arizona has proposed a "Health Kids Initiative," whereby school districts would receive federal funding to offer group-rate medical insurance for the more than 11 million children whose families earn too much to receive public health care but are not covered by any other health insurance (Dricks, 1992). The assumption is that schools can do the impossible—fill the gap left by dysfunctional families, lessened church influence, disintegrating neighborhoods, and overburdened social service agencies.

A Losing Battle

Some contend these social service supports are essential, but that the war will never be won. The underlying structure of local control and funding based on local property wealth will never result in a system of equity for all children. Unequal schooling therefore is seen as a way of perpetuating structures of economic inequality originating outside the school system. Although a system of common schooling was intended to provide a base of knowledge for all people, it was never designed to provide excellence for all students. Some believe there are many who do not want this system of injustice overturned since there is a need to have people at the lower end of the economic scale—America needs minimum-wage laborers. If indeed the system was built to reproduce or recreate the structures and hierarchies of existing economies, then attempting to reform schooling without reforming society may accomplish little. Greene (1991) writes:

> It is becoming more and more evident that the technical and economic disasters the schools are asked to allay are not of the kind that can be helped by education. . . . We have only to confront the widening gap between the desperately poor and the shamelessly [sic] rich—between the lives led by the homeless on the park benches and the lives lived by the "fortunate fifth," who consistently resist raises in taxes of the kind that might sustain the least advantaged. (p. 182)

Levin (1991b) concludes that educational interventions on behalf of the most disadvantaged populations not only produce large contributions to gross national income but also reduce imposed social costs (e.g., reducing crime and public assistance; improving the health of the population). One policy implication is that economic returns are maximized by investing in the educationally disadvantaged rather than in the advantaged. However, this argument would not be acceptable to the parent of a gifted child or to a legislator with a large percentage of middle-class constituents. As Levin notes, "This is a juncture where the economics of educational justice leaves off and the politics of educational justice begins" (p. 145). Although schools are being asked to do it all, most agree that limited resources make this task nearly impossible; a few note that it will never happen since it would too greatly disrupt our system of "haves and have nots." Others still content that these types of issues are being used as excuses because even wealthy school districts are not meeting the needs of their best and brightest students; competition and accountability are necessary.

One can view the 1960s and 1970s in American educational history as a time in which the attainment of equity rose to the top of the public agenda. However, critics now reflect that perhaps too much focus was on equity and not enough on excellence, especially concerning expectations. Although the War on Poverty did indeed target a great deal of additional revenues toward disadvantaged youths, it also resulted in programming, whereby the targeted students lived in a world of worksheets and minimal skills. Little thought was given on how to work best with youths from disadvantaged homes. During the 1990s equity issues have resurfaced, but with a greater focus on equitable outcomes and excellence for all students. Most agree there is a need to set high expectations for all disadvantaged youths and change mindsets regarding what these children can accomplish. Green (1991) writes, "If we ever really learned how to educate, how to teach persons regardless of the conditions of their lives, then we might not get more equality, but we would certainly gain in assurance that the resulting inequalities are not unjust" (p. 233).

Can Schools Do It All?

This chapter has reviewed just three issues out of hundreds that relate to education's role in society. Other controversial issues that could have been discussed include the issue of schools maintaining gender inequities; struggles with mainstreaming severely handicapped pupils into regular classrooms; battles over how to teach certain subjects (e.g., phonics versus whole language); controversy over what to teach (vocational education versus a core academic curriculum); recent debates over whether to require students to perform community service work prior to graduation (as currently mandated in Maryland); or whether the state should mandate multicultural education activities (as being considered in Florida). Bilingual education, desegregation, and disadvantaged youths were selected because they represent issues in which schools have been asked to help overcome environmental factors that could impede learning or, in one case, where they have been asked to rectify social injustices caused by segregation.

Although educators are seldom held in high esteem, most Americans consider education the most vital component of society as a whole. Throughout our history, as our country's economic competitiveness was threatened (first by the Russians after the launching of Sputnik and now by the Japanese as our automobile industry continues to lay off personnel), education becomes even more prominent. Can schools do it all? If willpower can compensate for limited resources and an educational system that was never designed to support all students, then the answer is yes. If a radical restructuring of schooling and societal supports as a whole are not successful, then the answer is no.

7

What Is the Future of the U.S. Educational System?

Current National Activities

In April 1991 President Bush and Secretary of Education Lamar Alexander unveiled a plan titled *America 2000: An Education Strategy*. Developed as a means to move the country toward the attainment of the six national goals, as listed in Chapter 4, the strategy has been a key policy debate topic since its release. For placing education high on the nation's policy agenda and attempting to rally state and community support for educational reform, the plan is being applauded by many. On the other hand, the specific details of the plan are under harsh criticism, both for what it proposes and for what it does not propose. Figure 7.1 summarizes the major elements of the national strategy.

The plan is in line with the new federalism ideal since it proposes little additional federal funding for education; responsibility for restructuring the educational system is firmly allocated to the states and local communities. Instead, a new "national" (not federal) role is prescribed, whereby national goals, standards, and assessments are to be developed as a means to focus the country's attention toward a common vision. The plan also proposes a national research and development

146

Track I—For Today's Students
· Set World Class Standards
· Develop American Achievement Tests; Encourage use of results by higher education and employers; Offer Presidential Citations for Educational Excellence; Provide Presidential Achievement Scholarships for needy students who excel
· Develop and publish school, district, state, and national report cards
· Promote public and private school choice; Provide Chapter I as vouchers
· Make schools the focal point of reform; Develop Merit Schools program; Enact "education flexibility" legislation to remove federal constraints
· Develop Governors' Academies for School Leaders and for Teachers
· Encourage differential pay for teachers; Establish an national honor's program for outstanding teachers
· Develop alternative teacher and principal certification programs

Track II—For Tomorrow's Students: A New Generation of American Schools
· Form the New American Schools Development Corporation to raise private monies and fund "Design Teams" to develop break the mold schools
· Encourage the formation of America 2000 Communities that develop a community-wide strategy to achieve the six national education goals
· Fund 535+ New American Schools (one in each congressional district) to utilize work of design teams or develop their own break the mold school
· Bring America on-line through extensive electronic networks

Track III—For the Rest of Us (Yesterday's Students/Today's Work Force): A Nation of Students
· Business and labor are to establish specific skill standards and "skill certificates"
· Promote one-stop assessment and referral "skill clinics" in every large community and work-site
· Use the federal agencies as an example to develop a program of skill upgrading
· Enact sound literacy and adult education legislation and set performance standards for all such federally aided programs; hold a major conference to develop a nationwide effort of program improvement

Track IV—Communities Where Learning Can Happen
· Encourage the establishment of America 2000 Communities that adopt the national education goals, develop a community-wide strategy to achieve them, design a report card to measure success, and plan for and support a New American School
· Maximize program flexibility by streamlining eligibility requirements, integrating services, and reducing red tape.

Figure 7.1. America 2000: An Education Strategy, Summary of Key Points
SOURCE: *America 2000: An Education Strategy* (U.S. Department of Educaton, Washington, DC, 1991)

agenda funded by private businesses, not the federal government. It calls for the creation of a nonprofit New American Schools Development Corporation to raise money and fund between 20 and 30 design teams; these teams, in turn would create plans for "break the mold" schools.

America 2000 also emphasizes the importance of grass-roots community support for educational renewal. It asks communities to declare themselves *America 2000* communities, take steps to meet the six national education goals, and report on such progress via report cards. The strategy also contains most of the components that have been discussed throughout this book—private and public school choice, differential pay for teachers, national standards, and high-stakes testing.

The plan calls for Congress to appropriate more than $535 million for the establishment of 535-plus New American Schools, one in each congressional district. Federal money is also recommended for the promotion of new state choice and alternative certification initiatives and to support several reward programs, including student scholarships and merit schools. Although it has not been specifically proposed in the plan, President Bush has also recently requested Congress to approve a major funding expansion for Head Start programs.

As of spring 1992, 32 states and hundreds of communities have declared themselves *America 2000* states or communities. The first national report card focused on the six goals was released during fall 1991. The New American School Development Corporation raised nearly $50 million, and 11 design teams were selected during May 1992 from the nearly 700 proposals received. Indeed, these proposals spawned major activity as diverse teams of educators, businesses, universities, and think tanks were quickly pulled together. Even many harsh critics of the overall *America 2000* plan developed proposals in the event the strategy succeeds (Olson, 1992b). On the other hand, as of early 1992, the U.S. Senate had rejected support for private school choice initiatives and was cutting proposals for funding the New American Schools (Miller, 1992).

Criticism is widespread and harsh. Shortly after release of the strategy, the William T. Grant Foundation compiled responses from 30 leading education policy analysts in a document titled *Voices From the Field* (1991). Many of these analysts continue to resist the inclusion of private school choice for the reasons described in Chapter 5. Others believe that the "American Achievement Tests," as initially conceived, would have been dangerous and still raise doubt about more recent proposals that call for a testing "system" rather than a single exam. They are concerned that the perils of poverty, especially within inner-city systems, were not addressed at all. Some noted that it will be impossible for some cities to help themselves without additional financial support. Many expressed dismay with the proposal to create new design teams, saying that many already struggling reform ideas should get addressed before inventing new ones. The lack of real focus on the retraining of teachers was also of concern.

Overall, many felt the strategies were too simplistic in nature (e.g., Presidential Awards; choice) and were part of a political agenda rather than an educational reform agenda. "*America 2000* is not a plan for American education but a plan for re-electing the President" (Orfield, 1991). Strong supporters of the strategy note that many of these critics have had little power at the executive level since the Carter administration and therefore resist the proposed changes (Doyle, 1992).

This brief review of the *America 2000* controversy alerts the reader to the types of educational reform activities most likely to drive our system for at least the next decade. Some believe that the entire initiative is dependent on the outcome of the 1992 presidential election. Others, however, believe that *America 2000* activities will remain part of the national and state debate because the plan is driven by governors and other reform leaders, not just the president's office.

A Vision

This book has analyzed an array of controversial policy issues currently being debated as part of educational reform agendas. These issues include national goals, a national assessment system, public and/or private choice options, performance-based student assessment, school rewards, state takeovers, educational warranties, teacher career ladder plans, decentralization of power, and schools as social service hubs, as well as many others. Although these topics were addressed separately, most are considered in tandem as part of comprehensive reform packages.

What will the future of schooling look like? In part, the answer depends upon which reforms are enacted within each of the 50 states and the success of these ideas. The country could imitate France's minimal distinction between private and public schools; or, it may take on certain aspects of England's system, where 85% of the money goes directly to the school rather than an intermediary unit. National standards and assessments would make our system much more like those of France, England, and Japan. Developing better work-school partnerships will push us closer to the German model.

However, most of the reformers in this country are not trying to mimic other systems, but are attempting to recreate a system that supports and builds upon our pluralist society. Most envision that the agrarian 9-month year and 6-hour day will become traditions of the past. The core year for students may still be 180 days, but these days will be spread throughout the year, with intersession course work offered. Schools will be linked electronically, and students will be involved in joint interactive projects with classmates around the globe. Computer data transfer will eliminate paperwork flow to the state department. Grade levels will also become obsolete in that student progression will be based upon mastery of content, not upon chronological age. Teachers will become responsible for students' learning for several years, rather than for a single 9-month period. As modes of instruction are modified, students will become active learners rather than passive listeners. In addition, greater linkages between schooling and the world of work will be recognized by educators and employers.

The school will become the hub of the community, open year-round from 6 a.m. to 10 p.m., at least 6 days a week. It will provide both educational and social service support for children and their families. Day-care and preschool will be provided for all children in need of these services. Schools, not districts, will become the focal point, with district personnel and governing boards providing only general leadership and technical support. Educators will not be solely responsible for all outcomes, but will work closely with other public or private organizations. Comprehensive performance-based assessments will have been developed, and policymakers, educators, parents, and students will utilize such data to make instructional and policy decisions.

Will it cost more money? Although this is a major source of contention, the answer is yes. Even if every current dollar now spent on administrative costs were to flow directly to the classroom, these funds would be insufficient to support the technology, infrastructure, and expanded salaries necessary to operate a year-round community educational hub. Higher compensation will be needed for teachers advancing up career ladders and/or choosing to work 11 months instead of 9. Because of the expanded salary opportunities and greater authority, teaching may become a highly respected profession.

The United States' world ranking in educational funding is another indication that additional funding will be necessary. Although critics disagree with their findings, work by Rasell and Mishel (1990) show that the United States' investment in education as a percentage of our gross domestic product during 1985 was lower than that of many other industrial countries, including Japan, France, and the United Kingdom. This is not to say that money is the answer, but that targeted funds will be necessary to make investments in retraining and retooling of our educational system similar to those made by many corporations. In addition, funds are necessary to provide services not currently provided for all students in need, such as preschool and extended schooling.

A Dream?

Is this just a dream? No and yes. No, in the sense that pieces of this vision are already in place in various schools and states across the country. Yes, in the sense that willpower and resources to achieve these major changes do not currently exist. This is partly because too few people are critical of their neighborhood school, and little trust exists among the various parties that are needed to create a vast social movement for change. As part of the initial reform drive of the mid-1980s, too many quick and simple solutions (e.g., choice) were bandied about by newspapers and many business leaders. Viewed as low cost/no cost reforms, they served to divide the educational and corporate communities; educators believed that business leaders did not really understand the structure of the educational system, while the latter believed educators were simply protecting their own turf. Although these feelings still exist across the nation, many strides have been taken to develop stronger partnerships between these two worlds.

Several major business organizations involved in educational reform have now developed comprehensive strategies that include many of the "silver bullet" reforms such as choice, but only as one of many activities. Most also acknowledge that reform will require increased resources. In addition, many individual educators, as well as teacher associations (e.g., AFT leadership), have come to accept that major change is necessary. However, as pointed out earlier, our educational system is large and decentralized. As a single individual, former Prime Minister Margaret Thatcher was able to initiate major educational reform in Great Britain because their national system is centralized. In the United States, it will require 50 state legislatures, 50 state boards of education, and more than 15,000 local school boards to enact such changes. Indeed, our state and locally controlled system was designed to make broad national changes almost impossible in order to protect the rights of individuals.

Even if the willpower is generated, available resources do not exist given the current economy. Although numerous studies demonstrate that a sound educational system will pay off in the long run, concern remains over short-term financing. Additional taxes are unlikely during a recession. On the other hand, if history repeats itself, once the country witnesses an economic upturn and reestablishes a world leadership position, educational reform may lose its importance, as occurred after the post-Sputnik reforms.

Finally, there will always be struggles over education's role in our society. This book has illustrated how difficult, if not impossible, it is to maximize each of four societal values: equity, efficiency, liberty, and excellence. The tug between conservatism and liberalism will always continue, as will the battle between vocational partisans and those advocating strong academic curricula for all students. Education's role relative to inculcating American values and citizenship will also remain controversial, as illustrated by the bilingual education debate. Consensus may never be achieved, even with the six national goals as a road map; even if it is achievable, some believe such consensus would be unhealthy in a pluralistic and democratic society. Instead, debates on an appropriate balance will always be a part of our diverse society—one person's dream system may be another's nightmare.

I close with a quote from the National Governors' Association (1990):

> Our nation is facing a major crisis in education, one larger and more significant than was realized even a few short years ago. . . . [Our country] has been propelled by a deep awareness that our economic competitiveness, the quality of American life, and the continued health of the democratic government depend upon the quality of public education and the knowledge, skills, and attitudes of our citizens. Yet despite the efforts of Governors and many other Americans from coast to coast, our nation's future is still very much at risk. Why hasn't more been achieved? . . . The answer is simple. While the states have been working to reform the system they have always had, technological and economic changes throughout the world, as well as social and demographic trends at home, have

overtaken these efforts and rendered our education system obsolete. Over the course of the next decade, our nation must better educate far more Americans, of all ages, to new kinds and higher levels of knowledge and skills than ever before. We must do this with an increasingly diverse population, many of whom face substantial economic, social, or other barriers to learning, such as the effects of substance abuse, teen pregnancy, or inadequate health care. None of our citizens can be written off. (p. 7)

These policy debates will continue as Americans struggle to create an educational system that will truly educate all children for the first time in our history. Nothing less will do.

References

ABLE Educational Foundation. (1991, November). *Arizona children at risk: A public strategy for reform and renewal of our schools.* Scottsdale, AZ: Author.

Alexander, K. (1991). The common school ideal and the limits of legislative authority: The Kentucky case. *Harvard Journal on Legislation, 28.* Harvard, CT: President and Fellows of Harvard College.

American Political Network, Inc. (1992a, January 10). Pennsylvania choice: Stand by for round two? *Daily Report Card.* Falls Church, VA: Author.

American Political Network, Inc. (1992b, January 15). Principals: Revise policy on school choice. *Daily Report Card.* Falls Church, VA: Author.

American Political Network, Inc. (1992c, February 11). Georgia diploma warranties: Legislation considered. *Daily Report Card.* Falls Church, VA: Author.

American Political Network, Inc. (1992d, February 14). Maryland: Governor Schaefer endorses choice proposal. *Daily Report Card.* Falls Church, VA: Author.

American Political Network, Inc. (1992e, February 14). Miami Op-Ed: Scrap attendance-based license revocation. *Daily Report Card.* Falls Church, VA: Author.

American Political Network, Inc. (1992f, February 26). One-stop: A new function for N.Y.C.'s I.S. 218. *Daily Report Card.* Falls Church, VA: Author.

Amsler, M. (1992). Choice heats up. *Far West Laboratory Policy Update, (2),* 1-3.

Anrig, G. R. (1985, November). The decentralization controversy. *Education Digest, 51,* 125-127.

Armor, D. J. (1980). White flight and the future of school desegregation. In W. G. Stephan & J. R. Feagin (Eds.), *School desegregation: Past, present, and future* (pp. 187-226). New York: Plenum.

Armstrong, D. G., Henson, K. T., & Savage, T. V. (1985). *Education: An introduction.* New York: Macmillan.

Barry, J. E. (1983). Politics, bilingual education, and the curriculum. *Educational Leadership, 40,* 56-60.

Barton, P. E., Coley, R. J., & Goertz, M. E. (1991). *The state of inequality.* Princeton, NJ: Policy Information Center, Educational Testing Service.

Bastian, A. (1989). Response to Nathan: Choice is a double-edged tool. *Educational Leadership, 47,* 56-57.

Bennett, W. J. (1992). *The devaluing of America: The fight for our culture and our children.* New York: Summit.

Berlak, H. (1992). Toward the development of a new science of educational testing and assessment. In H. Berlak, F. M. Newmann, E. Adams, D. A. Archbald, T. Burgess, J. Raven, & T. A. Romberg, *Toward a new science of educational testing and assessment* (pp. 181-206). New York: State University Press.

Berliner, D. C. (1992, February). *Educational reform in an era of disinformation.* Paper presented at the meeting of the American Association of Colleges for Teacher Education, San Antonio, TX.

Bradley, A. (1991, March 6). Low pass rate prompts review of Texas teacher test. *Education Week, X*(24) 5.

Brown Easton, L. (1991). *The Arizona Student Assessment Program (ASAP) as educational policy.* Unpublished doctoral dissertation, University of Arizona.

The Business Roundtable. (1990). *The Business Roundtable participation guide: A primer for business on education.* New York: National Alliance of Business.

Carruthers, G. (1990). *Sharing responsibility for success.* Denver, CO: Education Commission of the States.

Cavazos, L. F. (1989). *Education: The future begins today—Remarks prepared for delivery before the U.S. Department of Education Forum* [Press release]. Washington, DC: National Museum of Women in the Arts.

Cheney, L. V. (1991). *National tests: What other countries expect their students to know.* Washington, DC: National Endowments for the Humanities.

Chira, S. (1992, January 7). "Choice" can be a mirage as schools vie in market: Lessons from Britain. *The New York Times,* pp. A1, A9.

Chubb, J. E., & Moe, T. M. (1990). *Politics, markets, and America's schools.* Washington, DC: Brookings Institution.

Cohen, D. L. (1991, December 11). Maryland may tie welfare to "responsible behaviors." *Education Week, XI*(15), 21.

Cohen, D. L. (1992a, February 19). Learnfare fails to boost attendance, new study finds. *Education Week, XI*(22), 1, 20.

Cohen, D. L. (1992b, February 19). States move to link welfare benefits to personal behavior. *Education Week, XI*(22), 1, 18.

Coleman, J. S. (1991). Choice, community and future schools. In W. Clune & J. Witte (Eds.), *Choice and control in American education: Vol. I. The theory of choice and control in education* (pp. ix-xxii). New York: Falmer.

Cornett, L. M., & Gaines, G. F. (1992, January). *Focusing on student outcomes: Roles for incentive programs—The 1991 national survey of incentive programs and teacher career ladders*. Atlanta, GA: Southern Regional Education Board: Career Ladder Clearinghouse.

Crawford, J. (1988, October 30). Split tongue: Self-appointed guardians hide Official English's real agenda. *The Arizona Republic*, pp. C1, C3.

Crawford, J. (1989). *Bilingual education: History, politics, theory, and practice*. Trenton, NJ: Crane.

Cushman, R. F. (1976). *Cases in civil rights*. Englewood Cliffs, NJ: Prentice-Hall.

Darling-Hammond, L. (1991, November). The implications of testing policy for quality and equality. *Phi Delta Kappan, 73*, 220-225.

Diegmueller, K. (1991a, April 3). Troubled R. I. district becomes first to request state takeover. *Education Week, X*(28), 1, 25.

Diegmueller, K. (1991b, November 27). Budget concerns spur lawmakers to reconsider choice law in Massachusetts. *Education Week, XI*(13), 1, 19.

Donofrio, R. (1991). *Murphy School District's D.E.S. office*. (Available from Murphy School District, Administrative Center, 2615 W. Buckeye, Phoenix, AZ 85009).

Doyle, D. (1989). One-size-fits-all public schools derive from a 19th-century concept in need of updating. *The American School Board Journal, 176*, 27.

Doyle, D. (1992, March). The challenge, the opportunity. *Phi Delta Kappan, 73*, 512-516, 518-520.

Doyle, D., Cooper, B. S., & Trachtman, R. (1991). *Taking charge: State action on school reform in the 1980s*. Indianapolis, IN: Hudson Institute.

Dricks, V. (1992, February 18). McCain unveils health initiative. *The Phoenix Gazette*, pp. B1-B2.

Dunlap, W. H. (1991, Fall). The goal is control. *Agenda*, 24-26.

Edelman, M. W. (1973). Southern school desegregation, 1954-1973: A judicial-political overview. *Annals of the American Academy, 407*, 33.

Educational Research Service. (1990, June). Effects of open enrollment in Minnesota. *ERS Research Digest*. Arlington, VA: Author.

Educational Testing Service. (1990). *ETS policy notes: Testing*. Princeton, NJ.: Author.

Elam, S. M., Rose, L. C., & Gallup, A. M. (1991, September). The 23rd annual Gallup poll of the public's attitudes toward the public schools. *Phi Delta Kappan, 73*(1), 41-56.

Farrell, W. C., Jr. (1990). School choice and the educational opportunities of African American children. *Journal of Negro Education, 59*, 526-537.

Finch, L. W. (1989). The claims for school choice and snake oil have a lot in common. *The American School Board Journal, 176*, 31-32.

Finn, C. E. (1991). *We must take charge: Our schools and our future*. New York: Maxwell Macmillan.

First parents convicted under Chicago truancy crackdown. (1990, November 21). *Education Week, X*(12), 2.

Flax, E. (1991, December 11). Condom policies move up school boards' agendas. *Education Week, XI*(15), 8.

Fowler, F. C. (1991, October). *Challenging the assumption that choice is all that freedom means: A French case study*. Paper presented at the Annual Conference of the University Council on Educational Administration, Baltimore, MD.

George, G. R., & Farrell, W. C., Jr. (1990). School choice and African American students: A legislative view. *Journal of Negro Education, 59*, 521-525.

Gerstner, L. V., Jr. (1991, Spring). Sound the alarm. *Agenda, 1*, 61-62.

Goldberg, K. (1988, May 18). Vermont's "tuitioning" is nation's oldest brand of choice. *Education Week, VII*(34), 9.

Green, T. F. (1991). Distributive justice in education. In D. A. Verstegen & J. G. Ward (Eds.), *The 1990 American education finance association yearbook: Spheres of justice in education* (pp. 221-238). New York: HarperBusiness.

Greene, M. (1991). Justice and fairness in education: Paradigms, contradictions, and critiques. In D. A. Verstegen & J. G. Ward (Eds.), *The 1990 American education finance association yearbook: Spheres of justice in education* (pp. 173-194). New York: HarperBusiness.

Guthrie, J. W., Garms, W. I., & Pierce, L. C. (1988). *School finance and education policy.* Englewood Cliffs, NJ: Prentice-Hall.

Hanushek, E. A. (1989, May). The impact of differential expenditures on school performance. *Educational Researcher, 18*, 45-51, 62.

Havighurst, R. J. (1970, September). The unknown good: Education vouchers. *Phi Delta Kappan, 52*, 52.

Hayes, L. (1992, February). News and views. *Phi Delta Kappan, 73*, 489.

Hodgkinson, H. (1991, September). Reform versus reality. *Phi Delta Kappan, 73*, 8-16.

Jaeger, R. M. (1991, November). Legislative perspectives on statewide testing. *Phi Delta Kappan, 73*, 239-242.

Jalomo, R., Jr., & Bierlein, L. (1991a, September). *Statewide guaranteed tuition assistance programs: An overview of five states.* Unpublished manuscript, Arizona State University, Morrison Institute for Public Policy, Tempe.

Jalomo, R., Jr., & Bierlein, L. (1991b, October). *Kentucky family and youth resource centers.* Unpublished manuscript, Arizona State University, Morrison Institute for Public Policy, Tempe.

Katz, J. L. (1992, January). Ten legislative issues to watch in 1992. *Governing, 5*, 38-39.

Kearns, D. T. (1988, May 6). Our schools: A failing monopoly. *Arizona Issue Analysis*, (102). Flagstaff: Northern Arizona University, Barry Goldwater Institute for Public Policy Research.

Kearns, D. T., & Doyle, D. P. (1988). *Winning the brain race: A bold plan to make our schools competitive.* San Francisco: ICS Press.

Kirkpatrick, D. W. (1990). *Choice in schooling: A case for tuition vouchers.* Chicago: Loyola University Press.

Kirst, M. W. (1984). *Who controls our schools? American values in conflict.* New York: Freeman.

Langley, M. (1990). Educational vouchers vs. schools by choice. *The Delta Kappa Gamma Bulletin, 56*, 8-14.

Levin, H. M. (1991a). The economics of educational choice. *Economics of Education Review, 10*(2), 137-158.

Levin, H. M. (1991b). The economics of justice in education. In D. A. Verstegen & J. G. Ward (Eds.), *The 1990 American education finance association yearbook: Spheres of justice in education* (pp. 129-147). New York: HarperBusiness.

Lewis, A. C. (1991, November). Putting the public back into policy making. *Phi Delta Kappan, 73*, 180-181.

Lewis, A. C. (1992, March). The politics of policy making. *Phi Delta Kappan, 73*, 508-9.

Lieberman, M. (1990). *Public school choice: Current issues/future prospects.* Lancaster, PA: Technomic.

Lyons, J. J. (1989). *Legal responsibilities of education serving national origin language minority students*. Washington, DC: The American University, The Mid-Atlantic Equity Center.

McLaughlin, M. W. (1991, November). Test-based accountability as a reform strategy. *Phi Delta Kappan, 73,* 248-251.

Miller, J. A. (1992, January 29). Senate rejects private school choice proposal. *Education Week, XI*(19), 1, 26-27.

Miller, M. H., Noland, K., & Schaaf, J. (1990, April). *A guide to the Kentucky education reform act of 1990*. Frankfort, KY: Legislative Research Commission.

Moore, D. R., & Davenport, S. (1989). Cheated again: School choice and students at risk. *The School Administrator, 7*(46), 12-15.

Nathan, J. (1989a, July). Before adopting school choice, review what works and what fails. *The American School Board Journal, 176,* 28-30.

Nathan, J. (1989b, October). More public school choice can mean more learning. *Educational Leadership, 47,* 51-55.

National Alliance of Business. (1989). *A blueprint for business on restructuring education*. New York: Author.

National Alliance of Business. (1990). *Business strategies that work: A planning guide for education restructuring*. Washington, DC: Author.

National Center for Education Statistics. (1991a). *Digest of educational statistics 1990*. Washington, DC: Office of Educational Research and Improvement.

National Center for Education Statistics. (1991b). *The state of mathematics achievement*. Washington, DC: Office of Educational Research and Improvement.

National Commission on Excellence in Education. (1983). *A nation at risk: The imperative for educational reform*. Washington, DC: U.S. Department of Education.

National Governors' Association. (1990). *Educating America: State strategies for achieving the national education goals*. Washington, DC: Author.

National Governors' Association. (1991). *From rhetoric to action: State progress in restructuring the education system*. Washington, DC: Author.

National School Boards Association. (1992, January 8). *Report documents development and changing patterns in school desegregation*. Washington, DC: Author.

Negin, E. (1991, Spring). Choice: An idea that just won't go away. *Agenda,* 11.

Odden, A. (1991). *The changing contours of school finance*. San Francisco: Far West Laboratory for Educational Research and Development.

Olson, L. (1990a, June 13). Missouri school's reform: Getting better or "Messing around with a good thing"? *Education Week, IX*(38), 1, 8.

Olson, L. (1990b, October 3). One year takeover by state, cautious optimism in Jersey City. *Education Week, X*(5), 1, 20-21.

Olson, L. (1992a, January 15). "Supply side" reform of voucher? Charter-school concept takes hold. *Education Week, XI*(17), 1, 22.

Olson, L. (1992b, January 29). Bidders striving to make the grade in "new schools" competition. *Education Week, XI*(19), 1, 28-29.

Orfield, G. (1991). Choice, testing and the re-election of a president. In *Voices from the field: 30 expert opinions on America. 2000, the Bush administration strategy to "reinvent" America's schools* (1991). Washington, DC: William T. Grant Foundation Commission on Work, Family and Citizenship and Institute for Educational Leadership.

Pedalino Porter, R. (1990). *Forked tongue: The politics of bilingual education*. New York: Basic Books.

Pipho, C. (1991, November). Teachers, testing, and time. *Phi Delta Kappan, 73*, 182-183.

Pitzl, M. J. (1991, December 15). Attending private schools on public money opposed. *The Arizona Republic*, pp. A16-A17.

Pride, R. A. & Woodard, J. D. (1985). *The burden of busing: The politics of desegregation in Nashville, Tennessee*. Knoxville: University of Tennessee Press.

Ramirez, J. D., Yuen, S. D., & Ramey, D. R. (1991, February). *Executive summary: Final report: Longitudinal study of structured English immersion strategy, early-exit and late-exit language-minority children*. San Mateo, CA: Aguirre International.

Rasell, M. E., & Mishel, L. (1990, January). *Shortchanging education: How U.S. spending on grades K-12 lags behind other industrial nations*. Economic Policy Institute Briefing Paper.

Ratzki, A., & Fisher, A. (1990, April). Restructuring education in a German school. *The Education Digest*, 17-20.

Raywid, M. A. (1989). *The case for public schools of choice*. Bloomington, IN: Delta Kappa Educational Foundation.

Rinehart, J. R., & Lee, J. F., Jr. (1991). *American education and the dynamics of choice*. New York: Praeger.

Romzek, B. S., & Dubnick, M. J. (1987). Accountability in the public sector: Lessons from the Challenger tragedy. *Public Administration Review, 47*, 227-238.

Rothman, R. (1991, September 18). Debate on merits of public, private schools reignites. *Education Week, XI*(3), 1, 16.

Rothman, R. (1992a, January 29). Council calls for a new system of standards, tests. *Education Week, XI*(19), 1, 30.

Rothman, R. (1992b, January 29). Group urges "hitting the brakes" on national test. *Education Week, XI*(19), 30.

Rothman, R. (1992c, February 26). O.T.A. advises caution in move to national test. *Education Week, XI*(23), 1, 23.

Shanker, A. (1990, January). A proposal for using incentives to restructure our public schools. *Phi Delta Kappan*, 345-357.

Sheane, K., & Bierlein, L. (1991). *Open enrollment/educational choice: A national review*. Tempe: Arizona State University, Morrison Institute for Public Policy.

Shepard, L. A. (1991, November). Will national tests improve student learning? *Phi Delta Kappan, 73*, 232-238.

Smith, M. S., & O'Day, J. (1991). In D. A. Verstegen & J. G. Ward (Eds.), *The 1990 American education finance association yearbook: Spheres of justice in education* (pp. 53-100). New York: HarperBusiness.

Sommerfeld, M. (1992, January 15). Putting graduates under "warranty" gains favor in districts and states. *Education Week, XI*(1), 16-17.

Spring, J. (1988). *Conflict of interests: The politics of American education*. New York: Longman.

State Policy Research, Inc. (1992, February). School finance equalization. *State Policy Reports, 10*, 20-22.

Tifft, S. (1991, Spring). Ready, willing and able? *Agenda, 1*, 28-31.

Timar, T. (1989, December). The politics of school restructuring. *Phi Delta Kappan, 71*, 265-275.

Toch, T. (1991). *In the name of excellence*. New York: Oxford University Press.

Tucker, M. (1991, Spring). Getting down to business. *Agenda, 1*, 62-63.

Underwood, J. K. (1991). *Educational issues: Choice: Wisconsin style*. Madison: University of Wisconsin, Center for Educational Policy.

U.S. Department of Education. (1991, June 30). *The condition of bilingual education in the nation: A report to the congress and the president*. Washington, DC: Author.

van Geel, T. (1991). Equal protection and school finance: Bargained incoherence. In D. A. Verstegen & J. G. Ward (Eds.), *The 1990 American education finance association yearbook: Spheres of justice in education* (pp. 297-316). New York: HarperBusiness.

Weiler, H. N. (1990). Comparative perspectives on education decentralization: An exercise in contradiction. *Educational Evaluation and Policy Analysis, 12*, 433-448.

Weisman, J. (1991, December 4). Heritage Foundation turns up pressure on business groups to embrace choice. *Education Week, XI*(14), 12.

Will, G. F. (1992, January 13). A sterner kind of caring. *Newsweek*, p. 68.

William T. Grant Foundation Commission on Work, Family and Citizenship and Institute for Educational Leadership (Eds.). (1991). *Voices from the field: 30 expert opinions on America 2000, the Bush administration strategy to "reinvent" America's schools*. Washington, DC: Author.

Winfield, L. F., & Woodard, M. D. (1992, January 29). Where are equity and diversity in America 2000? *Education Week, XI*(19), 31, 33.

Wirt, F. M., & Kirst, M. W. (1989). *Schools in conflict: The politics of education*. Berkeley: McCutchan.

Witte, J. F. (1991a). *Educational issues: First year report—Milwaukee parental choice program*. Madison: University of Wisconsin, Department of Political Science and the Robert M. La Follette Institute of Public Affairs.

Witte, J. F. (1991b). *Educational issues: Public subsidies for private schools—Implications for Wisconsin's reform efforts*. Madison: University of Wisconsin, Department of Political Science and the Robert M. La Follette Institute of Public Affairs.

Wohlstetter, P., & McCurdy, K. (1991, January). The link between school decentralization and school politics. *Urban Education, 25*, 391-414.

Index

About the Author

Louann Bierlein is an Assistant Director at the Morrison Institute for Public Policy, Arizona State University. Overseeing the Institute's education and social policy studies, she works closely with Arizona and national policymakers as they attempt to develop systemic educational reform initiatives. Her key areas of analysis include at-risk issues, career ladder programs, school restructuring, parental choice, school finance, and the linkages between education and social policy.

At both the state and individual school levels, her recent work has ranged from serving as the research coordinator for Governor Symington's Task Force on Educational Reform to examining parental involvement concerns for a local school. Current major studies include overseeing the technology design component for a New American Schools Development Corporation grant as part of the Hudson Institute project; a 4-year longitudinal study of pilot programs for at-risk students; policy analysis of a statewide school restructuring pilot project; and the evaluation of a Head Start/public school transition project. She serves on an Arizona Joint Legislative Committee studying at-risk issues and is vice-chair of the State Board of Education Advisory Committee on Career Ladders.

Previously, Dr. Bierlein served as the Education Research Analyst for the Arizona Senate. In this position, she analyzed an array of educational policy issues covering K-12 through higher education. In this position, she also served as the state director for the Arizona Pilot Career Ladder Project.

She obtained her doctorate at Northern Arizona University and continues to teach graduate-level research courses as an adjunct faculty member. She began her professional experience as a junior high science and math teacher.